TWO GUYS HUNTING

Praise for *Two Guys Hunting*

"As a grade-school boy of very small stature, I was intrigued by my very tall and lanky classmate, Stan Tebow. Did I mention he was tall? Anyway, Stan was smart, studious, and fairly quiet. I was short, boisterous, and more interested in being the class clown. In spite of our differences, we had a common thread in our love for nature, the outdoors, and hunting. Soon, we became good friends.

"Fast forward to our sophomore year in high school. I still lived in the same house as our grade-school days. However, at age 13, Stan and his family moved to Alaska. So, when Stan came back to visit, I remember sitting in the "commons" of my high school, completely enthralled by Stan's stories of hunting in Alaska! I recall him talking about hunting Dall sheep and moose that kept me on the edge of the wooden bench.

"At that time, I couldn't see into the future to the point where Stan and I would rekindle our friendship, in Alaska. He was a successful insurance agent, and I became a freelance outdoor photographer and writer. Both of us made our homes in Wasilla, AK.

"Then, later in life, we both moved back to the greater Spokane, WA area and, for the third time, rekindled our lifelong friendship and our still-common thread of loving nature, the great outdoors, and hunting.

"I lived in Alaska for 17 years and have plenty of Alaska hunting, fishing, and photography adventures of my own. So, it is with great familiarity and firsthand knowledge of hunting in Alaska that I highly recommend you read Stan's book, *Two Guys Hunting*. These are true tales from a genuine Alaskan hunter and a dear friend of mine.

"Reading *Two Guys Hunting* is entertaining, educational, and stirs up so many fond memories of my own time hunting in Alaska. I tip my camo hat to you, Stan. Good job!"

—Lon E. Lauber,
Outdoor writer and photographer

"Stan writes with a strong sense of adventure, courage and lots of humor! He is truly a seasoned hunter and knows the country. I was raised in a subsistence hunting family in Alaska, and his read on Alaskan life is fun and accurate."

—Eric Jeglum

"Within these pages, you will find some of the best hunting and fishing adventures that Stan Tebow and his friends experienced throughout the vast Alaskan wilderness and waterways. This collection of stories will have you laughing one moment, and on the edge of your seat the next. How they made it back from some of these trips, God only knows. This collection will have you ready to pack your bags and take on the Alaskan outdoors yourself!

"The only thing bigger than these Alaskan adventures is Stan's heart! As someone who has had the privilege of accompanying Stan on many fishing trips out of Seward, he goes out of his way to ensure everyone's experience is first class! From the food to the accommodations and knowledge of the water, I would come back with coolers full of fish and memories to last a lifetime!"

—Chris Marok

TWO GUYS HUNTING

Bullets, Bonds, and Memories from the Alaskan Wilderness

STAN TEBOW

with

STEVE FLASCHER

Publishing support provided by
Ignite Press
55 Shaw Ave. Suite 204
Clovis, CA 93612
www.IgnitePress.us

ISBN: 979-8-9922512-0-3
ISBN: 979-8-9922512-1-0 (E-book)
ISBN: 979-8-9922512-2-7 (Hardcover)

For bulk purchases and for booking, contact:

Stan Tebow
stan.tebow@gmail.com

Library of Congress Control Number: 2024926691

Cover design by MotivatedDesign of 99Designs
Edited by Elizabeth Arterberry
Interior design by Jetlaunch

FIRST EDITION

In memory of James E. Ozimkoski

July 21, 1953 – June 5, 2024
AKA: Putz, Moron, Schmuck, OZ, Jimmy O.

What is a friend, anyway? It's a person who you trust, and confide in. A person with whom you can pick up right where you left off, no matter how long it's been since the last time you were together. It's a person who welcomes you into their home with no strings attached, and you welcome them. A friend that can be counted on to do the fun stuff, and the serious stuff.

*As a hunter, a friend is willing and caring. A person who puts aside fear just to be part of something bigger. He will pay extra money to take a cab to be on time for a fishing trip, when he got on the wrong damn plane. He is a person who makes you laugh and laughs right back with you. He can "take it," but he can also "dish it out." He once told me that if someone told me to haul ass, it'd take me two trips. Such is the banter among true **friends**.*

This man was our true friend.

May your shots be true in the happy hunting ground, Jimmy. Until we see each other again, "Adios."

Acknowledgments

To all the people who made these stories possible:

Jim Ozimkoski

James Buchanon

Jacob Buchanon

Adam Tebow

Judy Tebow

Cindy Flascher

Rob and Kelly Haag

John Lewis

Jeremy Brumfield

Bob Thompson

Cecil Roberts

Tim Benintendi

Greg Svendsen

Greg Manelik

Gene Yockey

Brian Cain

Brian and Leslie Bagley

Chris Marok

Table of Contents

Preface

As I wrote this book, it became apparent to me that it needed some explanation. I first met Steve when I was in high school and he was a new fresh insurance agent representing a national brand. He doesn't remember that, of course, because I was a kid, and I was there with my dad. Fast forward ten years or so, I was hired by the same insurance company. We ended up at the same social events and became friends. We each knew the other to be a hunter, but it was at Steve's 40th surprise birthday party we put together our first joint trip. Once we started, we discovered we had a chemistry for success. In fact, our winning streak of tagging at least one animal we were after, on every hunt when we were together, lasted 23 *years*! We each had other successful, and unsuccessful, trips with others, but when we were together, it was magic.

A couple of lessons learned from our experiences are worth noting here. When you find that kind of hunting partnership, it is an amazing thing. Each of you brings your strengths and talents together for a common goal.

In addition, if you haven't started writing down your adventures, do it now! This compilation of stories is but a few of our escapades in the wilds of Alaska. We could have had a much better accounting if we had written these stories down as they occurred. This book is dedicated to our families, who helped us process all the wild game and fish through the years, and it is for them this book is written.

Chapter 1

Farewell the First Time!

In Alaska, we have the opportunity to apply for random drawing permits to hunt various species of wild game. A few of them are rare and have been coveted by hunters for years. One of those is that of the northern wood bison. There are three primary areas in the state of Alaska where permits can be obtained for the magnificent beasts: Delta Junction, Copper River, and the extremely remote Farewell area. After the results of the draw were announced in 1990, we found ourselves in possession of one of these rare permits for Farewell. Stan drew it. After receiving the news, we set about making plans for this hunt. Having never flown to Farewell before, we weren't sure what type of air taxi service we could get, or what the cost would be. You see, Farewell is on the other side of the Alaska range and 160 air miles from Anchorage. Interestingly, you can get there by dog team, since the world famous Iditarod Sled Dog race goes through there, but we were short on dogs.

The dad of a friend of my son's said at one point that he knew of a guy that flew there all the time and he'd get me his phone number. I called and made arrangements, not only to fly out with him, but to rent a four-wheeler and a trailer he kept stored at the Farewell runway. Our hunt was starting to take shape, and the exciting day arrived.

When we met our pilot at the airport, we were escorted to a plane that looked more like a commercial airplane than an air taxi, but we didn't think too much of it at the time. As the years went by and we talked more about it, I'm pretty sure we were piggybacking on someone else's cargo run. At any rate, we were dropped off and pointed to a four-wheeler and a trailer of sorts next to the runway. Back in 1990, wheelers were not as sophisticated as they are now. Even by those standards, we were surprised to find a beat-up two-wheel drive, chain drive Suzuki 250CC wheeler and a Sears garden trailer. You know, the kind you use around the rose bushes in the garden, or perhaps to haul a small bale of straw.

The weather was sunny and we were excited to be loaded up. We decided I'd take the first shift driving while Steve walked. The idea was that we would switch back and forth often so neither of us would get too tired. Armed with guns, supplies, and paper topographical maps, we took off full of hope and energy. The trail out of Farewell was, for the most part, flat, wide, and smooth, so after a while we decided to double up and ride together. I am sure that the sight of the two of us on that itty bitty four-wheeler was something akin to 13 clowns in a Volkswagen.

At one point, about 3 miles in, Steve hollered at me to stop. It seemed the tires on our little trailer weren't meant for anything other than the green grass of a nice yard, as one had a stick the size of your finger sticking out of the side of it. Not to worry, though; we were experienced outdoorsmen and had a tire repair kit with us. No details left to chance. We had everything we needed! (more on this a bit later.) After repairing the tire, we pushed on. The trail was getting more narrow and not as well traveled the further out we went. Pretty close to dark, we came upon a small hill that the 250CC four-wheeler just wouldn't climb, pulling the little trailer. It notified us of its displeasure by blowing the drive chain. Must be time to set up camp!

We pulled all the gear out of the trailer and put up our new Cabela's Alaskan Guide Series dome tent. As Steve got the stove out and prepared to cook dinner, we made an alarming discovery.

We had plates, pans, a stove, and so on—all the necessary requirements for cooking a great meal. Note: I said "cooking" a great meal, not "eating." Remember the conversation earlier about two experienced outdoorsmen? About not leaving anything to chance? Well, some doofus (Stan) forgot to pack any silverware. Not to be discouraged, nor stopped in any way from taking nourishment, we found ourselves tucking into our meal with our hunting knives and freshly whittled spoons from the local materials God provided. If you've never spent a week eating every meal from a spoon carved out of a stick, I suggest you try it. It adds an earthly quality to your experience.

In 1977, the Bear Creek fire swept through the area, burning around 1,000,000 acres of Alaskan wilderness. The Iditarod mushers named this part of scorched earth the "Farewell Burn." When we were there in 1990, the small brush and ground plants had recovered, but there were no standing trees. The benefit was enhanced visibility. You could see for miles. The downside was the walking. There were burnt and partial logs laying crisscrossed everywhere, which required some concentration. A broken leg or seriously sprained ankle out there would be way more problematic than not having a fork for your beans.

We woke up on day two filled with hope and optimism that our experience would be rewarding and fun. After breakfast in the dark, we took off to different logs to perform the function that most guys do in the morning. While staring off into the distance, I noticed a dark speck that appeared to be moving and getting larger. As I watched the spot, it kept on growing, and, finally, I could tell it was a very nice moose. Since I had a bison permit, I thought my partner should harvest this moose, so I finished the job at hand and scooted up to the tent to retrieve Steve's rifle.

When I got to him, Steve was ready, having now spotted the big moose. We watched and waited while that crazy moose trotted a mile right to us and provided Steve with an easy shot right in camp, maybe 40 yards. That kind of shot that day. Get it? Shot the day? Oh well. We spent the rest of the day right there in camp, dressing out Steve's moose, which was a dandy. The rack measured 58 inches and had real nice symmetry and tines. Even the brow tines were long.

Steve's moose and first Farewell trip

The third day of the hunt, and our second in camp, we went out for what my good friend would like to call a "scouting walk." If I haven't mentioned this before, I should now. I've never been real athletic. I ran cross country my sophomore year in high school, firmly anchoring the tail end of the "C" team. The closest I got to varsity was sitting in the bus on the way to the race. I dropped 30 lbs in four weeks and was recognized as the guy at the back of the pack who was too stupid to quit. It was this dogged determination I brought to our hunts, rather than ability.

A couple of miles into our day, we saw a group of dark dots in the distance. Given the terrain and our hunting prowess, we determined this was what we were after. We put a sneak on about 40 to 50 bison. Bison are herd animals that leave a couple on guard while the rest graze. I'm not sure if they caught our wind, or, since we were the only things visible over 6 foot tall and moving, they just decided to be cautious. A couple of them started to move, stirring up the rest of the herd. They circled and took off running, just like something out of the movie *Dances With Wolves*. At 400 yards or more, there was no responsible shot, and we stood in awe of the rugged beauty of these creatures as they thundered down the burn.

About noon, we ran out of water. The topographical maps we had were based on surveys dating back to 1958. The string of pothole lakes we were following, and figured we'd tap into for our water, were all dried up. At 1:00 PM or so, we topped out on a knoll and spotted a lake at least a mile further in the distance. The decision was made not to go there for water, as it was just too far from camp and we had five gallons back there. Steve spotted a moose grazing in the water and suggested we set up the spotting scope and take a peep at it. He was a magnificent animal. His head would disappear and resurface with tender grasses from the bottom of the lake hanging out of his mouth and water cascading off of his 60-inch plus rack. He was safe from us this day.

After packing up the spotting scope and tripod it was jointly decided we had better head back to camp. We hadn't walked 100 yards when another big moose stood up in front of us. He wasn't spooked, nor did he run or walk off. He just . . . stood there. I looked at my buddy and said I'd be happy to go home with a moose like that.

"I'll help you pack him!" Through our years of hunting, my good friend said that many times in his unselfish bodily sacrifice to the cause.

BOOM!

Then the work started. We dressed and boned out that moose over the next several hours. We were young and stout back then, so we're carrying enough game bags to properly care for that much meat. After making a grid of logs to elevate and allow the air to circulate under and around the rest of the meat, we headed back to camp with the first couple hundred pounds.

Remember that part where I said we ran out of water? For those who haven't been keeping track, that was several hours ago, and now, loaded with meat, we were wanting water badly, and needing it more. When we stopped for rest breaks, we would pick the blueberries from the tundra for moisture. At one point, we found a deep hoof print from a big moose that had passed through, and, stripping our handkerchiefs from our necks, we soaked them, sucking the droplets of water from them like crazed mad men. Sometime after dark, we made it back to camp. We drank our fill of water and put the meat with Steve's moose and prepared dinner. Knowing we had survived this tough day, and with fried pork chops coming out of a skillet soon, we reflected on how very few people in the world could possibly be this crazy. Then we heard them coming!

We could see the glow of the headlights of a Honda three-wheeler with one rider, and a guy running behind it. Since we were camped pretty much beside the trail, our meeting was a certainty. The gentlemen stopped and introduced themselves as Gene, the older one, and Greg, the running man. Gene had a bison tag and had filled it earlier that day. They had just delivered their first load of meat back to their base camp, which was at Farewell

Lake. They had taken the float plane option to get to the hunting area. After a brief discussion, we invited them to join us for dinner and spend the night. Our tent was a six-man, so there was room, and it was around 10:30 PM—pitch dark. Little did we know this would start an acquaintanceship that would last for several years, or the excitement we'd all share together in the next few days.

After breakfast the next morning, we split up with Gene and Greg, headed back to pack more of Gene's bison and us to my moose. Somewhere around halfway back to my moose, we looked across a small valley to see Greg running full tilt toward us. He reached the top of the hill we were on and announced, "Stan! There's a group of bison over there. About ten of them, and we'll have to move quickly."

I looked at Steve, who said, "Go; it's what you came for."

I peeled my pack off and turned to follow Greg; he took off running again. He ran a few yards, looked over his shoulder at me, unsatisfied with my early progress, and snatched my rifle out of my hand.

He said, again, "We must move *quickly*!"

Boogety, boogety, he takes off like a freaking gazelle, with me plodding dutifully behind.

About half a mile of this behavior took us to a rise, where we could see Gene waving and pointing 30° to our left. Greg made the course correction and took off again. The top of the next rise gave us a fleeting view of the bison as they disappeared over the next hill. We ran to where we last saw them and combat crawled to the top of the rise. We were rewarded with a clear view of nine animals strung out, single file, with the largest bull at the back of the line. I settled my breath and touched off a 300 yard shot with my .300 Weatherby magnum, scoring one of my most prized trophies. Not because he was big by bison standards, but because of the work and excitement of getting him.

Gene and Steve showed up shortly, and after photos and handshakes, we set about the work of dressing out our third animal of this hunt. Steve and Greg went to get the rest of Gene's bison while Gene and I finished boning and bagging my bison. They arrived back to where we were just as we finished up. The four of us, loaded down with heavy packs, started back to camp just before dark. The pile of meat at camp was starting to get pretty big by now.

The next morning, it was agreed that Steve and Greg, being more physically able, would pack meat to camp, and Gene, with his three-wheeler, and I, with our dinky four-wheeler, would ferry meat out to both Farewell Lake for Gene and Farewell Runway for us. I had repaired the chain with some baling wire I kept handy (I came from a farming family). The wire was soft, so I had to be very careful driving so as not to strain the makeshift repair. With roughly 700 lbs of meat for each animal, we made several trips. I had to repair the chain multiple times.

The next day was more of the same, and all the meat was recovered, along with some great-looking horns and antlers. We said goodbye to Gene and Greg at the fork of a trail, where we went to the runway to wait for our plane and they went to the lake.

Our friendship with the guys who were strangers just days before lasted many years. Gene, we lost track of first, since he worked for one of those secret government agencies—pick your three letters—and was transferred back to D.C. Greg retired from the military and, last I heard, was guiding hunters in Russia. He spoke the language fluently. Greg provided us with an additional, yet costly, benefit. He turned us on to the superior pack frames at Barney's Sport Chalet in Anchorage and Swarovski optics. I had a three to nine Leopold scope on my rifle and thought it was pretty good. In fact, it is pretty good. Comparing it to my new 3 to 12 powered Swarovski, however, is like comparing a coloring book to the Sistine Chapel. Both Steve and I upgraded our equipment for subsequent hunts.

Looking back at the memory of this hunt, I can't help but think of the animals harvested, the hardships, and the friendships. All are key ingredients in the reason why we hunt.

Stan's bison

Chapter 2

The Dillingham Pillow

My buddy Steve played a lot of men's league basketball in town and, one season, he struck up a conversation with a teammate, Bud Hodson, who owned the TikChik Narrows Lodge. It's a very nice Alaskan lodge where you can be guided out during the day for world class fishing and then, in the evening, tell your stories as you tuck in for a five star dining experience and fine wine. So Steve and Bud got to talking about terrain and hunting and fishing out there. The topic of big moose came up, of course, and Bud confirmed there are huge moose in western Alaska, specifically in the Wood River area out of Dillingham. At our next dinner, Steve proposed we give this a shot. Always ready for an adventure with my capable friend, I immediately agreed. We then set about the logistics of making such a hunt.

Dillingham is a village in western Alaska 331 miles southwest of Anchorage. The two ways to get there are, if you exclude the primitive bog walking, air and sea. There are no roads to Dillingham from any other populated area. Since we are on the subject, the population of Dillingham Alaska is 2115. You won't find a Ritz-Carlton there. Fortunately, commercial airlines service the town. We booked through Alaska Airlines and traveled pretty light due to connections and timing, talk of getting a big one dominating our discussion.

We booked the air taxi through a local we were referred to, Rick Grant. Rick had a de Havilland Beaver on floats. I like air taxis to have clean planes. It demonstrates pride of ownership, and you can make the connection that if the operator goes to the trouble to make sure you'd be okay picking your sandwich up off of the floor and eating it, the maintenance logs will be just as tidy. Rick's plane was spotless. As we arrived at his office, we were a bit surprised to find some of the guys there muttering and making threats about our soon-to-be pilot. It seems they were less than satisfied with their experience, and if Google had been around, they'd have not provided a single five star review. We were then notified we'd have to drive to Lake Aleknagik, a few miles away, to get flown out. Not being familiar with this area, we simply did what we were told and loaded our stuff into the truck. After a mile or so, Rick told us we needed to make a stop. His wife had a flat tire. Once a more suitable rubber ring had been installed, we were finally ready to get to the plane and get to hunting.

The entire day was one of those gray, drizzly days where it's hard sometimes to determine where the clouds end and the horizon begins. It was this "gray soup" kind of late afternoon we flew off in. We've flown with many air taxis during our adventures, and, typically, the pilot will circle an area prior to setting you down somewhere. They are not guides and they don't pretend to be, but unless you know where you're going to go specifically for drop off, you're kind of at their mercy. Rick wasn't in much of a mood to talk due to the former disgruntled clients and then the wife's flat tire, so we were taken aback when, all at once, he cut the throttle and extended flaps for landing. No circling to see the lay of the land, just, "Here we are. I gave you the good spot."

Seemingly, this was for helping with the tire. As we unloaded, Rick's mood lightened up measurably. He showed us where there was a plywood floor erected so we could put our tent on it, and a canoe he kept there for his own use. He wished us well and took off for home and a warm meal. We hastily put up a tarp to cook under and my brand new Barney's Bomb Shelter tent, as I had lost my last tent to the wind in Kodiak the past year. It was still gray and drizzling, but Steve said, "Let's try this new GPS out and see how it works."

After turning it on, we set off for a short stroll to see how cool this new toy would be. It's to be noted here that my dad taught me always to have certain things with me when I went out in the woods: gun, lighter, flashlight, rope, TP, small first aid kit, pocket knife, et cetera. Since we had flown commercial, all of this stuff was still packed securely away in my duffel when Steve brought up the idea of this short walk before bed. In fact, we were still in our blue jeans and hip boots, not having yet changed into our hunting gear. This turned out to be the first—and last—time I have ever left camp without my stuff.

We wandered 50 yards or so and sat down on a log to check out the features of Steve's new GPS. Armed with the instruction manual, which we were fighting to keep dry, he started pushing buttons and checking out different screens. The technology was brand new, and certainly new to us, so we poked and played with it until almost dark. When it was decided to head back to camp, we got up off our logs and each headed in a different direction. After a very short discussion about whose directional instinct was correct, Steve said, "It's a good thing we have this GPS!"

He clicked a couple buttons and pointed. "This way."

I shouldered my rifle and followed happily since I was ready for a warm dry sleeping bag and a pillow. After 15 or 20 minutes, the arrow on the GPS made an immediate 90° shift to the left. Figuring we had walked past camp, we took off in our new direction. We did this several more times before we stopped and admitted we were totally lost. It was not mentioned in the instructions that the GPS may not get a good satellite lock under the dense cover of the forest canopy.

With darkness only a little while away, Steve pulled a short piece of surveyor shape tape from his vest pocket, tied it off on a scrub willow, and said, "This marks the spot where we know we are lost."

We went 100 yards and tied off with another bright piece of the tape, and then another 100 yards. No sign of camp or even the lake, so we went back to the original tape and repeated the process, but 90° from our original direction. By now, it was dark enough that seeing the tape was impossible and we knew this wasn't going to be a relaxing night. We found a real dense spruce tree with branches that came almost to the ground and crawled under it. With me at 6'3" and Steve at 6'4", our legs were left sticking out in the rain, but we had rubber hip boots on, so they were protected from the rain. Not the cold, though.

We tried to get as comfortable as possible in our natural little shelter and laid back-to-back to share a little bodily warmth. Needless to say, we didn't sleep well, and we were up at first light. On the third leg of our "we are lost" grid, we saw the lake and made our way back to camp. A nap was the first order of business and we slept for several hours. Sometime during the day, the rain finally quit and the sun came out. After changing into our official hunting gear, we pulled the canoe to the water's edge, then paddled down the lake to do a little scouting.

Toward the other end of the lake there was a rise in the otherwise pretty flat terrain. This hill was covered with downed trees charred from an obvious forest fire in the recent past. Steve spotted a couple of caribou, which we watched from a long way off. On the return trip, Steve pointed out a shallow valley to our left, where a creek may have run into the lake years before, and said he'd like to come back to that spot because it looked "moosey." The next day, we paddled over to the spot Steve had pointed out and followed a game trail off into the woods; around noon we came to a place where it looked like the ancient creek had deepened, or perhaps where a pool had formed. It was kind of a cut bank surrounding a depression in the ground that was maybe 10 to 15 feet lower in elevation than the ground we were walking on, roughly half the size of a football field, all covered in willows. The willows, we could tell, had been ravaged by the largest members of the deer family feeding on them. We decided to set up and call.

This is significant for a couple of reasons. The first, we had never tried calling moose before, and the second, because it worked! Man, did it work! A month or so before we left on this hunt, I read a story in one of my hunting magazines about how the old-timers would use a coffee can and a strip of wet leather through a hole in the bottom of the can to imitate certain moose sounds. It could bring the big bulls running. Not knowing what sound we were trying to achieve, really, we soaked our leather bootlaces in water from our Nalgene water bottles and pulled the string. This brought out the very best moose melodies a Chase and Sanborn coffee can is able to produce.

When I was 12 years old, my dad took me black bear hunting off the west fork of the Methow River in Washington state's Cascade Mountains. We had hiked a couple of miles up Trout Creek, deciding to take a lunch break around noon. While my dad told me the story of how, two years before, he had made this exact trek, sat on this same log for lunch, and shot a bear coming down the trail on the other side of the creek, I got our sandwiches out of my pack and leaned the old 30:30 up against the big log and sat down. I was seated on the other side of my dad, separated from my rifle. As he spun his yarn, he suddenly stopped and pointed to my rifle, asking if I thought it would be a good idea to sit so far away from it. I realized his point and retrieved my rifle, leaning it up next to my left leg before continuing to eat my sandwich. In about 10 minutes, I glanced over the creek and saw a bear coming down the same trail Dad talked about and, with one shot, collected my first big game animal. You'll see the importance of this story in a bit.

While working the Chase and Sanborn Symphony of music grunts, Steve whispered, "I hear something!"

I have worn hearing aids since the age of 21, so I just trust my friend when he says this.

Out of the brush hurls this huge moose! He was the biggest moose I had ever seen in the wild. He was fired up and looking to kick some other moose rival's ass! He jumped off the cut bank in one gigantic, full stride and bounded towards us, pulling up short in confusion when he spotted us.

It was Steve's turn to shoot first that day, but his rifle was still strapped to his pack. As the moose wheeled, about to run, and Steve fought to get his rifle clear of the straps, I scooped up mine from its bipod where it rested at my feet and shot the big old moose in the back of the neck, dropping him immediately. Thanks, Dad!

I don't know if you're aware of this fact, but the Alaskan Yukon moose is the largest of its kind, and this one was a dandy, standing 7 foot tall at the shoulders and sporting 71-inch antlers. It was a magnificent trophy. It would feed both our families well into the approaching winter. After congratulations and a lot of

laughter as we recalled the moose jumping down the embank-
ment, Steve said, "I hear another one. Let's get the call and mess
with him."

If you've ever doubted whether calling works, I will share this.
Not only did we call this next moose to within shooting distance,
he walked up to within 30 yards of us, stepping over the warm
carcass of his fallen friend (or adversary). The second moose was
at least 65 inches, and Steve's trigger finger was twitching like a
frog leg in a hot skillet. We had a decision to make. With a 1400
pound animal on the ground and a date for extraction with a seaplane looming, could we responsibly get both animals dressed
and packed back to camp in time? It was decided we could not.
The second bull lived to fight another day.

It took the rest of the day to dress and bag the beast we
had on the ground. We guessed pretty accurately, according to
the scale of Alaska Sausage, that we had a little over 700 lbs of
boned out meat in eight bags we now had to get back to camp.
The first load went out with us that day. Then we made two trips
the following day, with the last load coming out the day Rick
flew back to pick us up. As usual, my buddy Steve performed
up to his superhuman reputation by carrying a bag of meat *and*
the 71-inch rack through the brush. I put the pack on once we
reached the lake only to pose for a picture. Holy cow, he *carried*
that thing?

The trip out was not eventful, and we said our goodbyes to
Rick. Then we got on the jet, headed for home. After arriving in
Anchorage, we got the families together to cut and shrink-wrap the
whole moose. A few days later, I cooked up some of the steaks,
only to discover they were slightly tougher than the soles of my
Danner hunting boots. I called Steve to see if he had tried any of it

yet. He was just chewing a chunk of backstrap at that very moment. We took all of the meat to Alaska Sausage and Seafood the next day, where they turned our harvest into the best Polish sausage, hamburger, bratwurst, hot dogs, and other delicious treats. Nothing gets wasted!

The story above inspired the poem "The Dillingham Pillow." I am sharing it here. It should be noted that I presented this to Steve for Christmas on a piece of paper that said "Dillingham Pillow" that was stapled to a chunk of firewood.

A 71-incher

He carried *that*?

The Dillingham Pillow
by Stan Tebow

From the East they came in pursuit,
Of the biggest and baddest trophy moose.

It was an easy hunt, they were told,
Just look low and high among the willow.

Now these weren't just rookies, no sir,
They had many animals between them, to be sure.

The two hunters were veterans of many strange places,
And they had hunted with many, many strange faces.

After the flight, set up camp and then sup,
The two boldly set out to see what was up.

Only a few yards did they intend to go,
To try a new navigational aid so they'd know.

Just to get the lay of the land one said,
A little scouting walk to clear the head before bed.

They walked a couple hundred yards or so,
And sat down on a log to play with the new toy.

Now a navigational aid is to help you find your way,
Or so they thought and were heard once to say.

I'm sure the thing has many a good use,
But to these two proud men it was all just abuse.

In an effort to follow the arrow back to camp,
They walked in circles for hours until they got cramps.

Now as darkness began to fall on the two,
They had a little meeting to decide what to do.

You see, up until this point, and a little past,
They failed to admit they had flunked the test.

They were only going a few yards and had no gear,
And as hours went by, they thought of ones dear.

It was decided at last to hunker down for the night,
And a dense spruce tree to shed the rain seemed just right.

So they each crowded under the protective boughs,
And each had a root on which to rest their brows.

The roots weren't positioned even closely right,
So they tossed and they turned and they shivered all night.

They shivered and they shook until the early dawn,
The gray morning light showed them what they'd slept on.

Now later that day, camp was discovered
And a welcome sight, sleeping bags on cots there hovered.

The two went on to have a successful trip,
Moose were seen, and taken, and packed on the hip.

Only the two know what was endured that night,
As the wind howled through the trees and created fright.

But the confidence gained seems almost worth it,
And the lessons relearned they will never forget.

As memories of this trip fade into past,
Our night under the spruce tree will forever last.

Chapter 3

Only Two to Kodiak

In the fall of 1995 we planned what had become our normal trip to Kodiak for deer. The usual invitation went out to the usual suspects, only to find that none of our buddies could make it. Not to be discouraged, we pared down our supplies and, on the last Thursday of September, hopped on a commercial flight to Kodiak and were met by the van driver of Seahawk Air. It was great to see Rolan and Jo again and climb aboard the always pristine Beaver for our hour-long flight to Grant Lagoon.

The year before, I had shown up in not very good shape and failed to fill all my tags. My wife, at the time, chewed me out for this, and made it very clear that if I was going to spend money to go, I'd better not let that happen again. Of course, she had no idea what went into a hunt like this, mentally or physically. I was set to fulfill my end of the deal this year, anyway. I had been working out more and lost some weight in preparation.

After arriving and setting up our usual driftwood cook shack and Guide Series dome tent, we slept soundly, looking forward to the next day. We got up and, after breakfast, decided to hunt what we called the Big Valley. It's visible from camp but around the lagoon a fair way. There's the usual swamp and alder crossings before gaining altitude, but once you do, the visibility really opens up. About halfway into the valley on the left side is an exposed hogback that makes the ascent to the top easier. Since we hadn't jumped any deer on the way there so far, it was decided a trip to the top was in order. The bigger bucks always seemed to hang out up high, anyway.

This day was no exception. As we approached the top, we hunkered down so as not to skylight ourselves, and were rewarded with a nice view of two respectable bucks feeding across the top. We slid back down and pulled our packs off so we could be more agile. The bucks appeared to be feeding our way when we spotted them, so we decided to wait them out. Rifles ready, we didn't have to wait long. They popped over the skyline, within our sight at exactly the same time. I don't remember if we spoke, or we were so used to each other we instinctively knew what the other was going to do. At exactly the same second, two shots rang out as one and two nice bucks were harvested.

We set about the duty of harvesting every ounce of meat from these two. Since both shots were headshots, not a bit was wasted. Once the bagged-up meat was loaded on our packs, we decided to have lunch and enjoy the views that our lofty perch afforded us. Our lunches were pretty standard out there: sandwiches or sausage and cheese with crackers. Dinners were definitely not standard, and will be discussed later in a different chapter. With loaded packs, we headed back down the mountain. Since we were loaded, we decided on a more direct route straight down to the beach, as then the walk along the lagoon would be easier. Steve turned to lead and another buck jumped up out of the grass. Boom!

Well, now we had to peel our packs off again and dress out the third buck of the day. As we turned to do just that, a fourth buck peeked up to see what had just happened. I heard my good friend repeat words I've heard many times before: "I'll help you pack him." So I shot that one too.

By now, it's around 2:00 PM and we had two bucks down that had to be dressed and bagged. We laughed and joked as this was going on. Mostly to celebrate our good fortune, but also because of my wife's admonishment not to come home without filling my tags. Now we were testing our equipment and mettle; loaded with two deer each, we headed back.

Remember the part where I said I was in better shape this year? Well, not better enough! We got down to the lagoon after some serious brush busting but because the lagoon had closed off again to the ocean it didn't have an outlet and the water levels had risen to where there was no beach to walk on. The water was right up to the alders, which made walking miserable and wet.

I found myself getting really tired around 4:30 PM and told Steve I needed to rest. We found a kind of horizontal log in the alders and sat down. After a drink of water and a snack, Mr. Physically Fit tells me it's time to go so we can make it back before dark. I totally agreed. Unfortunately, my body did not. I pushed with my rubbery legs and stood up, right before my knees buckled and I fell face-first in the lagoon. The water wasn't deep, but I had two deer holding me under as I fought for air. I'm glad this happened before cell phones with cameras existed, or I'm sure Steve would have had to take a photo before saving my life. As I struggled, a big, strong hand grabbed the back of my pack and hoisted. Ah, fresh air!

It was agreed that we would tie a buck each up in the alders and retrieve them the next day. With lighter packs, we made it back before dark. I was able to change into my dry clothes and enjoy the warmth of dinner and a fire. With commitment already in front of us to get the deer we left tied up, the second day was a pretty easy one. We got the deer and spent the rest of the day messing around camp, securing driftwood for bonfires and getting our meat pole secured and ready for more. The third day, we awoke rested and decided to head to the second valley on the same side of the lagoon our friend Jim Ozimkoski named Elephant Buck Valley. The story here should be obvious. He saw a huge buck up there on one of our hunts but could never quite get a shot at him, proving again that big bucks don't get big by being stupid.

Steve and I were on our way over there from camp and, about 150 yards out, we saw two brown bears growling and circling each other. We took our packs off and got our binoculars, ready to watch what we thought was going to be a splendid territorial fight. Much to our surprise, a third bear stood up. More growling ensued, along with some serious swatting and biting. These were all about six- to seven-foot brown bears weighing roughly 500 pounds apiece, capable of breaking a cow's neck with a single powerful blow. As they circled and growled, we whispered back and forth, watching intently. All of a sudden, just beyond the trio, a huge brown stood up full height on her back legs. Yes, I said *her*. It turns out what we thought was going to be a bloodbath of epic proportions was just a teenage argument, and when Mama bear wolfed one time, all three obediently formed a line and, in single file, followed her off into the woods. What a sight!

After they left, it was time to press on. Walking on tundra hummocks is tedious and, at times, dangerous. Up one foot one step, then a three-foot drop into a hole the next. The good news is that tundra is soft when you fall, which happens on a regular basis. We headed into the valley but didn't see anything, likely because deer don't like brown bears much, and ours had just been through there. About three quarters of the way into this particular valley, the ridge on the right side descends to the back of the valley, making it a shallow, less steep approach to the top. Remember, big bucks are always on top. Up we went. Once on top, the walking is easy, the visibility great, and it just makes you feel fantastic.

With Steve in the lead, we started walking the ridgeline just off the top so only our heads would be visible from the other side. About 100 yards into this walk, he spotted a big buck and asked me if I wanted it. After a glance I said, "sure, he's a nice one." We don't shoot all the deer we see.

The buck was feeding with his head down, facing away, and when he raised his head, I settled my crosshairs on his neck just below his head. When I squeezed my trigger, I felt confident of my shot. The deer crumpled like a duck out of the sky. Steve looked at me and told me it was a nice shot. He went on to say that, since we were at the top and that deer wasn't going anywhere, we should walk a little further down the ridge to see what else was out there. So, after mentally marking this spot, we strolled leisurely down the ridge line another 300 yards or so. We were rewarded by the views, but no additional deer. Upon arriving back to where I had shot from, we looked down the slope and couldn't see my buck. He was gone!

The immediate thought was of the four bears we had seen earlier. These are the kind of thoughts that make those soft little hairs on the back of your neck stand at attention. We pointed out a grid, using a bush here, and a rock there, splitting up and moving in a zigzag fashion as we looked for my buck. The mountain, at this elevation, was covered in open rocky areas and low, almost knee-high brush with tundra. You wouldn't think it would be hard to see a deer. I was a little lower on our search grid, Steve was higher up when he yelled, "here he is." He followed that up with, "He's a pretty nice buck, Stanley, you may want to have him mounted."

Steve is one of the only people who's allowed to call me Stanley. Having saved my life a couple days ago and all, I wasn't going to complain. I walked over to within 30 yards of where he was standing, but I was directly downhill. As I started upward, and Steve downward, to my buck, the darn thing jumped up and ran straight at me!. I hollered, "I really didn't want him to come out of there!"

Images of me grabbing him by the antlers and bulldogging him to the ground rodeo style vanished faster than a drop of water on our camp wood stove. Instead, I dove for cover, rolling over and coming up with my rifle at the ready. When the buck turned in his rapid getaway, my second shot found its mark. He tumbled and rolled down the mountain—a long way down. Unfortunately, it was the backside of the mountain, and further from camp every tumble he took. We made our way down to where he lay. While dressing him out, we were able to determine my first shot went clear through the neck without hitting bone or blood vessels. The impact had just knocked him out. Loaded with my deer in my pack, we decided to go out a different way. We were now in what we call The Valley of the Moon, so named because the slopes are mostly void of vegetation. This is also the furthest from camp we hunt on this side of the lagoon. Since it is the furthest, and now midafternoon, we knew without voicing it out loud it was time to head back to camp. Off we trudged, Steve again in the lead and I, burdened by my pack, following behind.

We had gone about a half a mile or so when Steve sat down, waiting on me to catch up. As I breathlessly flopped to the ground beside him, I looked down the valley and saw a real nice buck looking at us. I whispered to Steve, "There's a buck."

He looked at me and, with a tone of resignation in his voice, said, "Yeah, I told myself if he was still standing there when you got here, I'd have to shoot it."

He then unstrapped his gun from his pack, took a good rest, and made a terrific 300 yard shot in the neck that dropped his buck like a stone. Unlike mine, his stayed put. We arrived back at camp in time for happy hour and dinner, tired yet feeling fulfilled from the blessings of the day.

That night, bad weather rolled in. We woke to dark gray skies and a lot of wind. We decided a shorter hunt was in order, so we went to what we call The Bowl. It is closer, and one of our favorite hunts. It should be noted that deer don't like wind much. It takes away two of their defensive senses, smell and hearing. I mention this not so much as science, but as the reason we didn't see diddly that day.

We did have a moment of humor at one point in the day. It started pouring rain and we decided to hunker down in some alders with our tarps to wait the squall out. We always carry 5 X 7 tarps to use when dressing out our deer to keep the meat off the ground and clean. I looked over at Steve, drenched, water running like a little river between us where we sat. He looked over and said, "Come out to the coast, we'll get together, have a few laughs."

Of course, he was repeating the line Bruce Willis used in the original *Die Hard* movie. That moment, it caused us both to break out in uncontrollable laughter.

After a while, we realized Mother Nature had no intention of giving up on this storm and we headed back to camp. What we found upon arrival was not good. I believe the west coast of Kodiak Island should be the place where all tent manufacturers test their product before releasing them to the public. There is something about a good storm in the Shelikof Strait that one should experience. We got back and discovered my brand new Cabela's Alaskan Guide Series dome tent flat on the ground. As we dropped down the last knoll of our return hike, we could clearly see the outline of our cots with sleeping bags underneath the wet nylon.

We got busy and stood the thing back up and restaked it, thinking it might be okay. We broke out the cribbage board and cards for a little bad weather entertainment. From the warmth of our cook shack, we could peek out and watch gust after gust of wind as it laid the tent flat, then the tent would quiver and spring back up. Finally, after a valiant attempt to quiver its way back to a dignified stance, the fiberglass poles started to shatter, one by one. The tent was done.

We were pretty philosophical about stuff like this, so we simply got our stuff and moved it into the cook shack. It was a little crowded, but functional, warm, and dry. I might mention we went on to tag out and have a very successful hunt.

Two to Kodiak

Chapter 4

Moose Camp

After I had hunted with Steve for a few years, I convinced my dad to allow my "brother from another mother" to join us in Dad's moose camp. I cannot reveal its location here, because as I write this, we are packing for another exciting and hopefully successful trip. My dad will be 90 years old in a couple of months, and he's still riding his four-wheeler up to our special campsite. Over the years he has built a tree stand that now looks more like a cabin on stilts. He spends the week there reading, napping, and calling moose. More often than not, he'll be successful simply by being patient, while Steve and I bust the brush and burn gas in our wheelers going from one meadow to another.

Since the Alaska Yukon moose is the largest member of the deer family, we go with the idea that one moose is enough to split between our two families. Where our moose camp is, there are size restrictions on how big the moose must be to be a "legal bull." A 50-inch spread across the antlers, or four brow tines on one side, are the requirements. Brow tines are the points that stick out the front of the rack over the moose's eyes beyond the main beam of the rack. The age of a moose and the quality of the food in their area can affect the development of the rack. After a moose reaches maturity, the rack size can actually get smaller as it gets older. The healthiest mature bulls, aged five to eight years, seem to provide the largest antlers. These are antlers, not horns, so they shed and grow them every year. It gives me a headache just thinking about it!

As I pointed out earlier, we can't just shoot any old moose with a set of antlers and field judging these things is critical. We'd rather pass on a close one than end up with one that doesn't measure up.

There are two things a hunter can do to get good at this field judgment. One is to find places where racks are displayed and practice guessing them for measuring accuracy. Number two is to invest in quality optics. I have a set of Swarovski 10 by 50 and 15 by 56 binoculars I use in the field. Yes, they are big and heavy, compared to small binos, but you can't shoot what you can't see.

One story I have about field judging comes from a year Steve and Dad were sitting in the tree stand and they called in a nice bull. They looked at it and decided it just wasn't big enough. Close, but no cigar, as they say. They got several good pictures of it and thought themselves lucky to have called in this moose and had some fun with him. It doesn't matter how many times you've done it before, there's always excitement as you are judging a close bull through your binoculars, hoping he's big enough or has the required brow tine count. So off walks this moose, and two evenings later, just before dark, my brother-in-law Cecil shoots it! A legal 52-incher. We headed over to help him dress it out, and it's the same darn moose! We verified it with the photos.

I want to note that this was the year Judy, my wife, came to moose camp. She did a great job riding her four-wheeler on some really rough trail. She also came and helped us dress out Cecil's moose. Originally, Judy thought she might be a little unnerved by the butchering process, but she ended up being more fascinated by how we do it for such a large animal. I guess her 30 years of nursing experience prepared her.

On a different year, we were riding one of our normal trails when Steve spotted a nice bull through the trees. We whispered excitedly back and forth about how we might sneak up on him. It was decided we would sneak quietly towards his flank and get behind him until we could work our way up the side and get a good shot. It was my turn to shoot that day. We executed our nifty (nobody uses that word anymore, so I'm bringing it back) moves. The moose turned away from us but didn't run. We were like ninjas, but dressed in camouflage rather than in black PJ's—or so we thought.

As we crept closer for a sure shot, the fellow turned his butt to us one last time. I say last time, because, from the rear, with its rack extending beyond his body the way it was, it looked big enough to me. I settled my crosshairs on the back of the neck just below his head. He was only 20 to 30 yards away, so not a difficult shot. One could speculate whether he was quite 50 inches or not. He was very close, but he did have four brow tines, so it made the tape stretch conversation a moot point.

The reason this particular moose is so memorable had nothing to do with the story thus far. It was more interesting as we dressed him out. The poor fella didn't run from us, because he already had his ass kicked that day. We discovered a penetration wound, likely obtained from a big antler, all the way into the left rear thigh, and his femur was shattered. He couldn't have run from us if he had wanted to. As we butchered him out, we said a little prayer of thanks, as is our tradition, but also included a special thanks that we could end his suffering life and save him from a painful death at the teeth of the wolves that winter.

In September of 2016, we found ourselves back in moose camp. Moose season ended a few days before we always planned our Kodiak deer trips, so we were fortunate to do both several years. Well, okay, almost every year. Did I mention we like to hunt? One of those mornings, we backed our wheelers out of the garage and turned towards the trail, having decided to go to a place we call the Killing Fields. Yes, we have names in moose camp, too! The garage is a 24- by 36-foot plastic tarp suspended over a log and draped back at an angle. We can pull under it so the machines are dry for the night.

Anyway, I backed out and looked across the meadow closest to the cabin and I saw a moose. It took me a split second to determine that it was what we call a shooter! I hollered at Steve, but he had seen it too. We started discussing how we could get close. We left the wheelers running rather than turn them off, thinking the change in noise was more likely to scare him than leaving them on. He casually strolled off into the woods and out of view and we decided on a plan to stalk him. We got close for a shot. I really don't remember who shot him, or what the measurement was, because that's not the important part of this tale. It's the gut pile.

There are quite a few grizzly bears in the area. Well, technically, they are brown bears, because they're within 50 miles of salt water. Anyway, we have a habit of sticking a stick in the gut pile of a moose that we kill with some surveyor's tape on it as a flag. This allows us to see if the gut pile has been disturbed from a distance. Bears don't like being walked up on while they are eating, I've been told. As we continued to hunt that week, we checked the gut pile regularly. Sure enough, one day, the flag was down.

If you have never walked up on a place where a brown bear has been feeding, I'll tell you: it's a mess. If they don't drag it off into the woods and eat the whole thing, they bury it and come back to it. In our experience, usually that is about two days later. When I say "bury it," I think you need more of an explanation to get the picture. They tear up the tundra for several yards in every direction. It looks like a job that a novice on a mini excavator could have done. Then they urinate and defecate on the pile multiple times. I'm guessing that adds flavor for later when they dig it back up and finish the four-star dining experience. Yummy!

We checked out the pile and decided the evening hunt would be spent watching this gut pile. Thinking the timing would be about right, at around 4:00 PM, we strolled over to a spot almost exactly 41 yards from the gut pile. We have rangefinders now. I found an uprooted tree where the root ball would provide protection from being approached from the back side. We didn't think that was likely, given the wind direction. Steve whispered over what he thought the bear would do if it came in on us that evening. "I expect he'll skirt around those dense spruce trees, and when he stops to eat, we'll have a good shot."

At about 8:15 PM, Steve whispers loudly, "Look!"

Is it actually possible to whisper loudly? Anyway, we see this blob of fur running around the edge of the spruce trees. Loping along, not sprinting. The darn bear did everything we had predicted. Well, except one thing! He didn't stop to eat. As soon as he saw us, he bolted right at us! The son of a gun jumped over the gut pile at a dead run.

It's funny how, sometimes, life turns into slow motion. I remember my gun being up and ready, pulling all the slack out of the trigger, getting ready for a follow up shot. It was Steve's turn to shoot first, since I already had two of these things. I kept wondering, why doesn't he shoot? Then, as I figured I had waited long enough, I started applying pressure to the trigger, expecting the break in a split second. Boom!

It was Steve's shot. The bear simply stopped! I don't mean it got scared and ran away; I mean he stopped. Folded up like a dead bird out of the sky. Steve's shot had hit home just a little below the bear's right eye. Pretty incredible, considering a bear's head moves a lot when it runs. I believe in early chapters I've mentioned Steve's propensity to make headshots.

The bear plowed into the ground and across a log. Steve's .300 Weatherby Magnum not only killed the bear, but stopped all forward momentum. It didn't roll. It didn't even twitch. The distance to the bear was 21 paces. Close enough, since they can run 35 mph. It is funny how training and practice take over in a time of need. Cold execution was what was necessary, and that's how we reacted. About three to five minutes after we confirmed the beast was dead, we started laughing nervously and joking like a couple of seventh graders that just kissed a girl for the first time.

Steve, Jim Tebow, and Stan at moose camp

Steve's grizzly

In 2017, my great nephew came to camp along with my son, Adam. Adam had a history of hunting up there, but hadn't been to moose camp in several years. Something about life. Going back to college to become an accountant, having kids, that sort of thing. It was a fun weekend and we called up a 55-inch bull that Steve let Connor, my nephew, shoot.

As with our deer camp, moose camp has places that are named. There's Bear Meadow, The Killing Fields, Camp 1, Lower Meadow, and Twin Meadows. There is also the Plywood Bridge, the Log Bridge, Alpine, and several lakes that, if I named them here, you'd be able to find our spot. One year, Steve and I were riding up to Alpine. It is a pretty steep trail as you gain altitude, then it sort of plateaus on a small bench. I was in the lead, with Steve right behind me, when I looked off to my left and saw a bull moose lying down at the base of an alder group 50 yards away. I stood straight up on my foot pegs and turned to holler at Steve, but he, too, was already standing up on his foot pegs, staring. We slowly stepped off our four-wheelers, leaving them running. Then, we did the combat crawl from our wheelers to a little knob in the tundra that's a couple of feet tall and maybe 40 yards from this moose.

At first, we thought, *too small*, since his palms were deceivingly narrow. Then I said to Steve, "his beams are really long and he flares out at the top."

Back and forth the discussion went for at least five minutes, while he just laid there, looking the other way. If you figure 9 inches between the ears, and the beams are longer than that . . . Finally, I said to Steve I was convinced he was 50 inches. Just barely, but 50 inches. I told him if he didn't shoot the fellow, I was going to. It was his turn to shoot first that day, so he fired and the moose just rolled from head up to head down. Killed instantly.

We walked up to the moose who, when he went dead, dug one antler into the tundra so we couldn't see it, and my first words were, "Shit, what have we done?"

Looking at the one pitiful palm sticking up in the air, I wondered how I could have been so wrong. We called Dad and had him bring his game trailer and a full complement of game bags, for work was about to begin. We also made sure he brought a tape measure. In the meantime, trying to feel better about ourselves, we wrenched the head up so we could get to see both sides. Steve cut a string the length of the rack. Then I pulled out a dollar bill and began inchworming the string and counting out loud, the premise of this being that, since a dollar is 6 inches long, we should be able to come close to an actual measurement. Well, the technique has a lot of room for error, and we weren't totally convinced of the results. We had to wait for the tail of the tape, as they say. Because of the flare at the top of the rack, he ended up measuring 52 inches! Whew! He looked more like a Texas Longhorn than a Yukon moose. Our field judgment was good.

We learned another lesson on the descent from Alpine. Don't load a whole moose in one trailer behind one wheeler. The moose almost ran over Dad on the way. I can almost see how that would have looked in the paper: "Old Man Killed by Dead Moose—Karma!"

Dad's riding skills prevailed, and no old men were harmed in the making of this story. The funny thing came to me as I write this. I wonder what happened to that rack? Dad has the racks of many of our moose on his shop. This one was pretty ugly and didn't make the cut, I guess.

The Killing Fields are so named because of the success we have had there. One year we called in a dandy 58-inch bull. The photo we took of Dad and me with him turned out to be so good that I used it for several years in advertising for my insurance agency. The next day was the final day of the season, and we decided to go back to the Killing Fields. The reason escapes me now, because we normally don't go right back where we've just killed one. Anyway, it turned out to be the right decision. Early in the afternoon we called up another legal bull. Steve got this one, and it was within 50 yards of the one we got the day before. It didn't have as pretty a rack, but it still made for good eating.

As the years have passed, moose camp has gotten more metropolitan. We take a small generator now, and have a multi-phone charging station, electric lights, a big three-burner propane cooktop, and Dad has extended the top bunks for Steve and me. They were originally 6 feet long and a bit short for us.

Dad is a master at getting things built. He built an entire outhouse that I pulled up to camp in the winter behind a snow machine—snowmobile, for all of you non-Alaskans. He built a sled just for this function. A different winter, we hauled his pre-fabricated tree stand up and put it all together that fall. That was Steve's first year there. Dad can build just about anything.

Several trips, my brother-in-law Cecil has been in attendance. He's an excellent shot and is very good at calling moose, too. He got the only moose we killed this year after he and Steve called it in to the Killing Fields. I watched and took pictures. You see, I am no longer an Alaskan resident. I purchased a black bear tag and a non-resident license. I have made several stalks on black bear up at moose camp and have always zigged when I should have zagged. After Cecil shot his respectable 56-inch bull, last year, I did have a hand in getting it bagged and in the trailer.

The year before, I couldn't go because I was moving. Steve went with his son in law, Rob, and my Dad. They saw several moose, but none were legal until the last day. It was late, and Rob asked Dad if he wanted to head back to the cabin for dinner. Dad declined, not wanting to give in before the total end of season, which would be at dark. Well, the old guy still has it. About 15 minutes after Rob headed back to the cabin, Steve spotted a legal bull at the far end of the meadow. Dad told Steve to shoot it, but he told Dad to go ahead. After hearing the shots, Rob called to verify they had one down. He brought meat trailers and game bags and it was midnight when they got back to the cabin for a celebratory rum and Pepsi. Not bad for an 88-year-old.

Stories will continue for at least one more year, I'm guessing. We just installed a new ladder at Dad's tree stand a couple of weeks ago, and he has this idea that it would be really cool to shoot a moose next year, when he turns 90.

Chapter 5

Hello Farewell, Again!

Our first trip to Farewell for my bison and our two moose was 13 years after the Farewell burn. On this trip, Steve was the lucky recipient of the bison permit, and it was 13 years after our last trip. Mother Nature has a way of healing, and the scrub brush we were able to navigate easily 13 years prior had turned into dense brush 30 feet tall. Visibility was horrible compared to the first time, limiting us to hunt trails and meadows.

Mother Nature also has a sense of humor. When I shot my bison in 1990, it was hot. We were wearing T-shirts and doing everything we could to elevate the meat and make sure it was cooled. Fast forward to 2003 and temperatures were hovering around 0 degrees Fahrenheit at night. It was difficult to keep our water bottles from freezing solid.

Let me back up here. If you read the earlier installment of our Farewell adventures, you remember we didn't know what to expect and ended up with some substandard equipment. Not this trip! We rented a Sky Van out of Anchorage International Airport to fly two good four-wheelers and trailers out this time. Plenty of transportation capabilities for the four guys. Our lofty ideas, of course, were to duplicate our trip of 1990, where Steve and I harvested two nice moose and a bison. Back on the ground with camp set up, we had prepared for the first day of hunting.

Present and accounted for were four eager and capable out-doorsmen: Steve, Brian, Jim, and myself. Steve and Brian paired up the first day, while Jim and I set off down the famous Iditarod

Sled Dog trail on my trusty Honda four-wheeler. We hadn't gone far before we spotted a meadow we thought we should check out more carefully. No sooner had we stopped the four-wheeler than, *boom*, the sound of a magnum rifle shot split the cold morning air, followed by the immediate slap of a slug finding its mark. I looked at Jim and he said, "That was quick, I guess we better go help."

Two able-bodied guys can dress a huge moose, but it is much easier with four. Off we went to help out. We arrived a few minutes later. After congratulations to Steve for his 50-inch moose, we set about the knife work. Jim grabbed a leg opposite me and on the first cut around the knuckle, I saw him turn his knife over, changing directions, cutting towards himself. When his knife made it through the skin of this Alaskan Yukon big bad boy, the surgically sharp blade of Jim's new knife plunged into his own leg, right into the meat of the quadricep muscle. My good friend had made a serious boo-boo.

I told him to stand up and pull his pants down so I could assess the seriousness of the injury. He did and squeezed his leg between trembling fingertips, more surprised and embarrassed at this time because of our body's ability to mask pain with shock, and blood poured out. I grabbed the bandanna from my neck, a multi-purpose tool, really, and had Jimmy lay down, wrapping it tightly around his leg while hollering to the other two hunters.

By 2003, technology had improved and gotten more affordable. For the first time in our hunting years, we had a satellite telephone back at camp. It was decided that the fastest of us would go get it. That was still Steve, so off he ran back to the four-wheeler, which was parked a hundred yards away, and then rode off to camp. I dug out my GPS and turned it on waiting for the LCD screen to comply ever-so-slowly in the cold temperature. We had Jim quiet and lying down with his feet elevated, covered in coats. He was still shivering and we were more than a little worried about shock and hypothermia.

As soon as Steve got back with the phone we had to teach ourselves how to dial it. He called his office because he knew he could get a hold of someone there. The battery and the phone were cold, so we weren't sure how long it would last, nor how long we would need it to. Connection was made with the State Troopers who turned us over to the rescue coordination center at Kulis Air National Guard Base in Anchorage. They asked for our GPS coordinates and told us to "build a fire" so they could ascertain the wind direction and velocity. They also asked us to brush out a landing spot for a helicopter.

50 minutes later, we were fighting the prop wash of a full-sized Black Hawk helicopter. Our spot was not nearly big enough. We started doing the bushfire stomp because blasts of air from the huge gunship were scattering the aforementioned fire. There wasn't a decent landing spot close by, so a body appeared at the door and was lowered to our location by a basket on a long thin cable. He was a strapping young medic who quickly went about his business checking over our friend.

Jim had been with us on many hunts in the past, and I'm not sure why he goes. You see, he's terrified of heights and he doesn't like to fly. Both sensations were about to be tested to the limit as they strapped him into the man basket and lifted him up into the helicopter hovering above. I thought I could hear him yell above the prop wash roar, but I'm sure I was mistaken.

You could almost hear him scream!

When the heroes in green come and rescue you, there are no side trips. This includes going back to camp to get your wallet, so Jim ended up in Anchorage at the hospital where he received some stitches. He found himself almost 400 miles away from home with no wallet, money, or credit cards. Not only was he going to be fine, he was playing golf within a couple of days while we were doing the thing good friends do. Brian took a picture of himself naked in Jim's sleeping bag to send to him, and we relieved him of the Crown Royal he managed to smuggle into camp in a Nalgene water bottle. You know, those things are very durable.

The next day found *us* one man short in camp to continue using the age-old buddy system, so it was agreed that we would stay together and climb one of the nearby ridges to see what we could see. We got our binoculars out and scanned the dense forest for signs of life. After an hour or so, Steve said he was watching a spot that looked almost black. It wasn't moving, but it looked out of place, so he thought he'd go get a closer look. Brian and I continue to scour the hills and valleys, looking.

What seemed like 15 minutes later, *bam*! I pulled my high-powered glasses down from my eyes and looked at Brian. He smiled and said, "Well, let's go!"

We grabbed our gear and headed down in the direction Steve went. We got down on the flats and couldn't see him, but he heard us and hollered from his location, about 100 yards to our right. We should have been able to see the sun's reflection off his teeth, given the size of a smile we were greeted with.

Steve's bison and second Farewell trip

Bison are herd animals, for sure, but the biggest bulls, the herd bulls, often separate themselves from the herd when it's not breeding season for some quiet R&R. Steve's was such an animal, much bigger than the one I got 13 years prior, but not quite as big as a small school bus. After congratulations and photos, plus a little prayer of reverence, we set about the task of harvesting this magnificent animal the way he deserved. We took our time so as to not miss an ounce of meat. He provided some of the best eating you have ever known (there's a reason these beasts were almost hunted to extinction without proper control).

We had only 200 to 300 yards to get the meat to the trail through some pretty dense stuff, so rather than load packs, we each grabbed a game bag of meat, hugged it to our chests, and walked. After three trips of this, we had all of the meat out to the trail, and Brian and I set off to get the wheelers. Back at camp, we elevated the meat for air circulation and hung a tarp higher over it in case of rain. It was still freezing at night but warming up some during the day, so rain was possible.

Feeling rather good about ourselves, we set off the next morning with songs in our hearts from a successful hunt, and a sat-phone call to our buddy Jim, who was fine and playing golf. It was agreed that elevation was a ticket for success, so we went to climb a different ridge to see what we could see from there.

Shortly after reaching the top, Brian said, "You see those white spots way out there?"

We looked through our binoculars and we were rewarded with the sight of a huge bull moose. His palms looked like sheets of plywood in the distance—a distance we estimated to be just over a mile. There are two ways to get close to a moose like that. One is to stalk it. The other is to have him come to you. After our hunt in Dillingham, both Steve and I became students of calling moose. The morning air was still and we knew the sound would carry, so we set up to call. It isn't difficult, really; you just have to talk moose! We grabbed a big stick and started beating the brush and a dead log nearby.

Have you ever seen a science fiction or military movie where the satellite dish turns and follows some undescribed signal? That's what this big boy's antlers looked like when the sound finally reached him. He turned and started towards us, never running, but at a steady walk, as we watched in delight. Every now and then, he would stop and tear up a small tree with his antlers, a sure sign he was interested and open for business. As he got closer, much closer, we realized we didn't really have a plan! Within moments of this realization, he disappeared at the foot of the small ridge we were on. We now had a big angry moose coming at us, but no visibility.

Fortunately, with his rack that big and the brush pretty dense, we had another sense kick in. We could hear him, and he was about 20 to 30 yards beneath us. When we heard him turn and bolt down the hill, Steve and Brian jumped up and took off in hot pursuit. I stayed up on the ridge in hopes of catching a glimpse and maybe waving a direction to my buddies. It wasn't, but a couple of minutes before the report of Brian's .338 magnum split the silence, followed immediately by the telltale slap that could only be a successful shot. I picked up my pack and headed off in the direction of the shot.

Upon my arrival, I discovered Steve and Brian standing over the trophy moose. It was even more impressive up close. The rack measured 66 inches, and it was attached to the body of a mature Yukon Alaska moose, which ranged from 1200 to 1600 lbs. Like all hunts I've been on, when the gun goes "bang," the work begins. The next several hours were consumed by harvesting this big guy for our freezers. Fortunately, we didn't have to pack this moose terribly far to the trail—only about three quarters of a mile. That allowed for a nice short rest on the return as we made multiple trips back and forth.

The next day was our final day in camp, and we had a plane to meet late in the afternoon. We scurried about taking down camp and loading the two trailers full of gear and meat. We didn't feel the need to make two trips because we had good gear with us this time. Only about 10 miles separated us from the runway where our chartered Sky Van would swoop us back to civilization. With the machines loaded down with two huge moose and a bison, we realized it would need to be a slow trip.

About 3 miles in, we traversed a side slope down to a small gully. The downhill tire on one of the trailers was stretched to the point it rolled off the rim. We had to stop and unload everything to get the weight off and address our issue. We always travel with a small quantity of tools in anticipation that not everything will go as planned. This trip was no exception. We used one of our ratchet straps around the tire to apply enough pressure to seat the bead of the tire back on the rim. I purchased and brought along a small 12-volt air compressor that plugged into the bayonet-style recep-tacle of the four-wheeler. Although not fast, it sure beat a bicycle tire pump, and wasn't any heavier than one, either.

The rest of the trip was textbook. We met our plane on time, and our families picked us up at the airport upon arrival. Jim was fine and we all enjoyed the meat that long Alaskan winter!

Chapter 6

Fishing Is Just Hunting on the Water

Kiwi II

For about 15 years, I owned a 38-foot boat in Seward. After years of adventures with smaller boats, my friend Jim DiMaggio convinced me to "get real." I put my name on the 40-foot slip waiting list and, four years later, was awarded my slip. As I was walking the dock after just doing my happy dance over my new slip, a guy was hanging a sign that said "for sale" on a boat called the Papa Bear.

I told him I was interested, so we took the boat for a test drive and cut a deal that very day. As luck would have it, he was good friends with my hunting partner Steve—I'd had no idea. I have to admit, getting rid of that boat and getting the next boat was one of my biggest mistakes. My youngest son, Aaron, has been calling me Papa Bear since he was a small boy. I even have a Papa Bear tattoo on one shoulder. When the motors started giving me trouble, though, I put the Papa Bear up for sale and bought the boat across the dock from it, called the Lunacy. We renamed it to the Kiwi II, since I married Judy, who was born in New Zealand, and she was my Kiwi I. It was also a 38-foot boat at the water line, 43 overall. We enjoyed the ability to get off the dock for three or four days at a time and do some fishing, whale watching, and bay camping. Usually we had at least one guys' trip per season.

Boating season in South Central Alaska is pretty short. Like the trips to Kodiak for deer, we didn't keep dates or very good track of the trips. On one such trip, Steve, Jim O, and I were headed to Thunder Bay. We spent the first day fishing for halibut and rockfish without a lot of luck and headed for Taz Basin to anchor up for the night. Taz Basin is one of my favorite spots to water camp because the entrance is very narrow, and, once inside, the water is flat as a table top. As a captain, it is one of the places I could sleep like a baby and never worry about slipping anchor.

Well, we heard a distress call in a conversation with the local Coast Guard from a sailboat stranded in Thunder Bay. It seemed his kicker motor had quit and he needed a tow to open water so he could catch some wind. We knew we were headed that way, but stayed out of the conversation because we weren't sure when we would get there, and it wasn't a dangerous situation for them.

The sailboat indicated he was fine on supplies and was in no danger. We decided to head that way after fishing a few holes on the way, and as we rounded an island, there was a Coast Guard cutter pulling into Thunder Bay to offer help for the stranded sailboat. We were happy that the sailor was getting help, and a bit selfishly happy that it didn't involve us.

Steve was at the helm of my boat when a booming voice came over the radio. "Unidentified vessel headed to Thunder Bay, what are your intentions?"

It appears the Coast Guard isn't fond of a boat following theirs into a dead end bay, responding to what could have been a decoy distress call! The thought, of course, never crossed my mind— something I was able to convince the captain of the big white and orange gun ship of. In an embarrassed, feeble voice, I said, "we are just going fishing."

After a couple of radio exchanges in which I'm sure I sounded pretty stupid, he said, "Carry on."

Yes Sir! We anchored up about halfway into the bay in 150 feet of water and caught several halibut. As we fished, we watched the efficient protectors of our waters hook onto the sailboat and drag it several miles out into the open ocean to catch sail. Towards the evening, we went around the corner up to the head of the bay where the water is very protected. We anchored up about 40 feet in and proceeded to pour our cocktails and prepare BBQ steaks on the back deck. Customarily, if we hadn't limited out yet, we would drop a bait over the side and keep it just above the bottom in a rod holder. On many occasions, this practice has been successful, and we would pick up a big halibut cruising through the shallows looking for an easy meal. In this case, it was Steve's, and the result was an 80-pounder! Jimmy O was pretty upset it wasn't his! What great fun!

If you leave Seward and head east far enough, you get to the western entrance of the beautiful Prince William Sound. We went there a lot. On the way, you pass Johnstone Bay, as well as others. The neatest thing about Johnstone Bay is the glacier that formed it is still there and actively calving chunks of ice into a river that flows into the bay. By the time they get to the ocean, the ice chunks aren't usually very big, but you can spot them if you know what to look for. We loved harvesting them for our coolers and, more importantly, our evening cocktails. Have you ever had a cocktail with 10,000 year old ice in it? It lasts a long time.

One trip, my wife, Judy, Steve, and I headed to Susie's Hole. It should be noted that, like hunting camp, fishing places have names, too. I never met Susie, but the guy I bought the Papa Bear from was a friend of Steve's, and was kind enough to leave the GPS coordinates for all his fishing hotspots loaded for us in the navigational system when I bought it. The first time we fished Susie's Hole, we were rewarded with some great fishing, so we returned several times. On this particular trip, we got set up and Judy decided to crawl below and take a nap. She left her line in the water and Steve was close to her rod when it decided to bend double and start bouncing. "Big fish" was the first thing he said, so he hefted it from its rod holder. Yes, it was! After a battle of a good half hour, we shot it and brought it on deck.

When the fish hit the deck, Judy woke up. She ran up and promptly tried to claim her fish. "But it was on my rod!"

Steve was having none of it and he laid claim to the 93-pound halibut. It's funny how the fish hitting the deck woke Judy up. What about the two gunshots?

On one of our joint adventures, both couples were present: Steve and his wife, Cindy, and Judy and I. We went east again and harvested ice in Johnstone Bay. We fished a couple of GPS spots their son-in-law, Rob, gave Steve to try. We overnighted in a place called the Fox Farm, so named because it apparently was the site of a 17th century Russian fox farm for the fur trade. Anyway, we were anchored up, enjoying the prep work for the evening meal and a glass of really good Cabernet, when a whale was sighted cruising pretty close to shore. It was headed our way! Whales are really common where we go, and close encounters are always special. This gray whale surfaced right between our boat and the shore. He/she wasn't more than 20 feet from the stern swim step. It was so cool to watch the huge, gentle creature slip so smoothly through the water. It hung around us for several minutes before moving on.

Not all boating adventures are tales of great weather, big fish, and whale sightings. On one guys' trip, it was *totally* not that way. Steve, Chris Marok, Jimmy O, and my dad, Jim, joined me for what was planned to be a four-day adventure. We were about an hour out of Seward when I noticed one engine overheating dramatically. We had sucked up a huge jellyfish into the cooling system, which blocked the cold-water intake. I shut the motor down and opened the hatch. I was greeted with black inky smoke. I ran to the forward hatch to open it and get air flow to clear it out while barking orders at the others. I had to see if we were on fire or not! Thank God, we weren't.

After the smoke cleared and the engine compartment cooled, I fired up the unaffected motor and we limped back to the dock. I was reminded and glad of my prejudice about boats. I always liked twin diesel motors. Diesel doesn't explode, and twins, well, there are two of them! We were down not only for that weekend, but the rest of the entire season while the starboard engine was rebuilt.

You know, before big boats, we still had fish. For resident Alaskans, there are a couple of salmon dip net fisheries. One of the most famous—and dangerous—is the Copper River. We tried it the first couple of times by just driving over and finding a spot that looked good. We got a few fish, but it was real hard work for the filets. We learned the best fishing is in the narrow part of the canyon, and there are charter operations that will take you and drop you off for 12 hours. They are backed up a lot of times, so we developed a technique of going midweek and at night.

Summer daylight hours allowed us to leave home in the morning, driving the four and a half hours to Chitina where we could catch the charter. We would then get put on a 6 PM charter and fish until we got tired. We would usually fish until midnight or so and then lie down on the rocks for a nap if we hadn't limited out yet, then get up and fish until the boat came the next morning. We did this for several years and got a lot of delicious Copper River red salmon. We had the chance to take a couple to Emeril Lagasse's Restaurant in New Orleans on a reward travel trip for our company. He made an appetizer out of one for our group, and took the other one home!

I started my love affair with saltwater running a 14-foot aluminum skiff my dad had when I was a young lad. He upgraded to a 16-foot one a couple of years later (Ooh, aah!). I had the opportunity to buy a 22-foot Reinell from a client that became a good friend for $5000, so I jumped at the chance. It needed work. The motor was almost brand new, but the outdrive needed to be rebuilt and the gas tanks had rotted out. My neighbor built a couple of custom aluminum gas tanks for me and I rebuilt the outdrive.

After repairs, Steve and I loaded up and headed to Valdez. The trip was about five and a half hours from my house and went without incident. Well, as far as we knew. We arrived in Valdez and got out to launch the boat, only to realize the spare tire holder had bent all the way to the ground without breaking. The result was the spare had dragged on the pavement for several miles and worn entirely through. The sidewall was as flat as you can possibly get.

We ran the boat out to Galena Bay and had a good day of fishing. Steve landed a 65-pound halibut. We anchored for the night and kind of slept in the narrow V berth the boat had. Sometime in the early morning, we woke to a strange sound. It sounded like a low but fast buzzing sound, followed by a thump. It kept repeating over and over. It was a poor little hummingbird that happened to fly in through one of the windows we left cracked open for ventilation, and he was trying to get out. Unfortunately, he chose a closed window for his escape. With a pair of baseball caps, we were able to redirect the little fellow and he flew happily away. We had several fun trips with the Little Sprout, so named because of its yucky cream and green color scheme used by Reinell in the late 60s and early 70s. I believe this was the only trip though that Steve was on with me on this vessel.

At other times, prior to being my own captain, we'd take a paid charter out of Homer. One of our friends turned us on to a particular captain because they had a great time with him, and he worked hard to put them on to fish. This was Captain Rob Zolo, and he worked for Inlet Charters at that time. Three or four years straight, we would put together a "six pack" of folks and book his entire boat. On one such trip, our good friend Jimmy O flew from Fairbanks to Anchorage and was going to fly a local small airline to Homer to join us. This was prior to 9/11, and the small airline required you to go on the tarmac and get on the plane. We got a call from Jimmy that he was in Kenai, a totally different town. Yep, he'd gotten on the wrong plane. Jim hired a cab to drive the remaining 80 miles, and made the charter just in time. The cost per pound of the filets on that trip went up for him a bunch!

Stan and Steve with a 153-lb halibut

Steve and I have been hunting and fishing successfully together for a long time. We have had successes with others as well, so this is not intended to be a total accounting—just a few of the stories of the things that we did together. I can't thank my "Big Brother" enough for instilling in me the mindset, "do what it takes to get what you came after!"

Chapter 7

Bear Stories

The following are two stories we felt needed to be included, even though we weren't together for them.

In the fall of 1997, my son Adam was 13 years old. He had been hunting with us a few times by then, and enjoyed being outdoors. We were hunting with my father up at moose camp, before there was much "camp" to it. Three generations of Tebow guys, just seeing if we could scare up a legal moose. Dad had an accident a month or so earlier and was nursing a broken back, so it wasn't intended to be a real physical hunt.

Late one afternoon, we set up on a large meadow several hundred yards from camp. Having had success with the coffee can and a leather shoelace in Dillingham the year before, I was calling regularly, hoping to sweet talk a bull moose into joining our little party. Adam, being 13 years old, was going through the snack pile pretty quickly. Just before it got too dark to shoot, we decided it was about time to pack up and head to camp. I turned around to face the tree that the three of us were leaning against and started stuffing gear and empty snack bags into my backpack. All of a sudden, Adam cried out, "Dad, bear!"

I spun around and locked eyes with a big brown bear. When I did, he turned towards us and came at a dead run. I grabbed my .338 Winchester Magnum and time slowed down. I concentrated on his right front shoulder and squeezed off a shot. My aim was true, and the bear stood up on his hind legs. He growled and was throwing slobber as he rocked his head from side to side.

Boom! Adam got a shot off. At his age, I was proud of him for not freezing and actually getting some lead in the air.

I racked another cartridge and got ready for my next shot. As the bear dropped back down onto all fours, I took aim and squeezed off another shot, figuring I'd hit him square in the chest. I had done such a good job with the shoulder shot that when he landed on his front paws, he crumpled down just enough that my chest shot ended up hitting him in the back of the head: game over!

"What did you get?" Dad hollered over. He was on the other side of the tree, facing the other way and had no idea any of this was happening until the first shot rang out.

I yelled back, "Bear!"

He scrambled over and asked where the bear went. He wondered if I had just wounded him. I said, "No, he's right there!"

Dad was looking off in the distance, not looking down. "Dad," I said, "he's right there."

"Oh shit," came the reply. Twenty strides!

It was decided I'd go back to camp and bring a four-wheeler to use the headlights while we skinned out the bruin. By now, though, it was pitch dark out. Even with my flashlight, I couldn't find camp. After an hour of looking, I decided to head back to the bear. I had been flagging my way with surveyor's tape. Dad and Adam had a nice fire going and had started skinning. I helped for a while, but we were all tired, so we curled up for the night.

The next morning, early, we finished skinning and loaded the hide and head in my pack. It took both Dad and Adam to help me stand up, it was so heavy. In the daylight, the trail was much easier to follow and we discovered I was on the right track the night before. I had turned around about 70 yards from camp. If I had just gone a little further, we would have had a more comfortable sleeping arrangement.

The bear "squared out" at 8 feet 6 inches. Big for the area, and respectable anywhere. The meadow is now known as Bear Meadow by everyone that hunts in the area, and it is the site of Dad's tree stand.

Stan's grizzly

Steve's Polar Bear
Written by Steve

As I was growing up, my dad always told me it was better to be lucky than good. This quote was proven correct in 1972. My roommate Roger Bray and I put in for polar bear permits and we both were lucky enough to be drawn in the state lottery system.

Roger was working on one of the oil platforms in the Cook Inlet and his boss was Eldon Criswell. Eldon had a good friend and they agreed to take us on our polar bear hunt for the grand sum of $500. Eldon's friend and pilot was John Graybill. John was a guide and had lots of experience on other bear hunts.

We left Anchorage on the 2nd of April in two Super Cubs (small private planes known for their short take off and landing abilities) with a destination of Kotzebue. It was a long flight of 547 miles. Especially when you are flying at only 90 miles per hour. My job along the route was to keep an eye open for wolves, lynx, and wolverines. At that time, it was legal to shoot these from the air, but we didn't find any in open areas.

After spending the night in Kotzebue, we loaded back into the Super Cubs and headed toward our hunt base camp in Point Hope, Alaska, which was 150 miles away.

After landing, we checked into our accommodations at Ms. Rock's Hotel. It was very rustic, to say the least. The beds were old Army cots separated by blankets hanging from the ceiling. The bathroom consisted of a "honey bucket" that they would take out and empty on the sea ice when it started to fill up.

The next morning, we flew out over the Bering Sea ice with nothing between us and Russia except more ice. The way you would hunt polar bears was by flying over the ice until you came across bear tracks, and then follow them until you found a bear. Once you found a bear, you would follow them to see what direction he was traveling and try to find a smooth landing area out in front of him so you could put a stalk on him.

Again, my luck held up, and I won the coin toss to determine who would shoot first. John and I landed, and the bear continued straight toward us. While we waited for the bear to get closer,

Eldon and Roger continued to circle above until we shot the bear. Everything worked perfectly and I had my trophy of a lifetime.

Later that afternoon, we found another bear for Roger. As Eldon landed, he slid across an ice heave and busted a ski strut on the plane. Roger got into place and shot his trophy.

While we were circling above, some fog came in and we built up some ice on our wings, which can be very dangerous. Coming in to land, we were only 15 to 20 feet above the ice. The plane stalled suddenly and we slammed into an ice floe, bending the propeller and fuselage of John's plane.

So, here we were with two planes down, stuck out on the polar ice! After taking care of Roger's bear, it was decided to take the ski strut off John's plane and put it on Eldon's. At that point, we had one plane flyable, but it was too late to get back to Point Hope. We were all going to have to sleep on the ice!

We had one sleeping bag in each plane for emergencies, so Eldon and Roger got them and slept in the plane. Meanwhile, John and I spent a long, cold night sleeping on the ice between two polar bear hides. Brr, *brr*! Needless to say, we didn't get much sleep that night. We did wake up when we heard Eldon fire up his plane, which was about two hundred yards from us. John and I crawled out from between the hides, which were frozen solid. We waved as they flew over and headed to Point Hope. As they flew east, towards the sun, we were both hoping that we would see them this afternoon. What made that such a tough problem is that the only navigational equipment in the plane was a compass. Unfortunately, when you are above the Arctic Circle, as we were, compasses don't work! You just have to fly by the "seat of your pants."

There was nothing for John and me to do except gaze to the east, looking for a plane headed our direction. At around 2:00 PM, we both heard the whine of an upper cub engine heading towards us. We were both excited when we could tell it was Eldon and now, the only question was whether we could repair John's plane enough to fly it back to Point Hope.

Eldon was amazing! When he got to Point Hope, he was able to find a person with a vice so he could bend and straighten the propeller. He was also able to fix the ski strut, and he brought back several two-by-fours that we would use to straighten out the fuselage. Once we put the propeller back on, we tried the engine to make sure it would start and John could fly it. Everything was okay. We cut the fabric skin on the plane so we could bend and try to straighten the plane. After taping the holes with "Super Cub Tape," John was ready to try it. John told me to get in with Eldon because he wasn't sure what was going to happen. He said that, once he was airborne, he was headed to Point Hope. John took off and we were able to speak with him on the radio as he flew. He was fine, except for having to constantly make course corrections to the left due to the crooked fuselage.

After making it back to Point Hope, John grabbed the bear hides and we walked over to a local native's home. The lady of the house was going to "flesh" the hide, which is a process to get the rest of the meat and fat off the hide. She would sit on a stool, holding the hide in her teeth, and use an ulu to scrape the meat off the hide. An ulu is a sharp curved blade with a bone handle common in the arctic. Her charge, for this tough work, was a bottle of whiskey per bear hide.

We loaded up the next morning and flew back to Kotzebue, where I caught a commercial flight with all our gear. That made it easier on everyone.

It was truly a great hunt for a 22-year-old kid who was really lucky!

Steve's polar bear

Chapter 8

First Elk Hunt

On Afognak Island, Alaska, there is a small band of Roosevelt elk. They were transplanted there in 1929 after being captured in 1928 on the Olympic Peninsula in Washington state. Fish and Game felt the weather and conditions were similar enough that the eight calves would flourish. Estimates of the herd size now are around 840 animals, and Alaska Fish and Game issue limited draw permits to manage the size of the herd. Getting drawn is special.

As with most of these permits, once you are drawn, the logistics have to be figured out. It is said that only 50% of those actually drawn for this hunt go. Primarily, this is due to the remoteness and expense. We went with our longtime friend and bush pilot, Rolan Ruoss, and Seahawk Air.

Rolan set us down on a freshwater lake just over a steep ridge from a salt water bay. There are no facilities there of any kind, so we set up camp right by the lake for ease. That turned out to be a rather bad idea.

The lake had an outlet stream that clearly connected to the salt water. This was evident by the late season salmon we could see swimming in the shallow water of the lake's edge.

After setting up our tent and stretching a tarp to cook under, we turned in for the night. Darkness brought on the expected grogginess and a deep sleep kicked in . . . *until*!

Steve and I both sat bolt upright in the tent after awakening with a start. What caused this rude interruption of our much needed beauty rest? *Ursus arctos middendorffi*. The great Kodiak brown bear!

We could hear him thrashing through the water very near our tent as he chased the salmon in the shallows. Once he had one in his powerful jaws, he'd come up on shore and devour his prey. At one point, he was close enough we could smell him, and when he shook like a wet dog does, the water sprayed the side of our tent. All we could do was lay there with our rifles at the ready and listen while the beast ate his fill of sockeye salmon sushi. Not much sleep happened after that, and the next morning, we decided to move the camp up a small hogback a couple hundred yards away from the lake, correcting our "rookie mistake."

Early the third day, we found a steep but reasonable trail up the mountain to a "saddle" at the top, a place my good friend Steve had declared to "look like elk country." He has this habit of making me go uphill, usually against my legs' desire. As we crested the top and started to follow a trail that revealed itself there, I paused to catch my breath and looked back down the trail. About 50 yards behind us was a dense little clump of spruce trees, and looking out of it was a nice bull elk. His neck and shoulders were all that was visible and he looked just like a shoulder mount already done at the taxidermy.

I whispered urgently, "Steve, come shoot this elk."

It was his turn to shoot first that day. It didn't take him any time to find a solid rest and send a fatal shot on its way.

Neither of us had done any elk hunting before, or any research about the Roosevelt wapiti. We were both amazed at the body size of this beautiful animal. The Roosevelt elk are the largest of the four types of elk found in North America, and this was a fine specimen. In fact, it was like walking up to a downed moose—800 to 1000 pounds on the hoof. We processed the meat and bagged it up. It took us all the rest of the day and the whole next day to get it all back to camp. We had pulleys and rope with us and suspended the meat up in the trees high enough to keep it from being taken by a big brown fuzzy bear.

The morning the plane was scheduled, we not only had to take down camp, but also all the bags of meat, *and* transport it all back to the lake. This was certainly more of a sprint than a marathon.

Once again, Seahawk Air showed up on time and we were blessed with another successful trip. The elk meat was a fantastic treat all winter.

Chapter 9

Second Elk Hunt

At some point I don't remember, we started putting in for party hunt permits. This simply means if one of your party gets drawn, the other guy gets the same permit. That's how we ended up on Afognak Island for the second time on a wonderful elk hunt, trying to repeat our last experience, or at least part of it. We went back to the same lake. We carried our gear up to the beautiful campsite on the hogback we discovered years before. In attendance were Steve, Jim O, and myself. We had two permits this time. A lot of the details on this hunt aren't totally clear, like which days we actually saw elk, how far we walked, etcetera. I do know we got robbed! Not our camp, but something maybe more serious.

We were walking along and Steve said, "get up here, Stanley!" I tend to be at the back.

He pointed through some pretty dense brush and there was an elk standing facing us full on. He was at full attention, but couldn't see us through the brush. At least, not yet! I snuck up to a close spruce tree and took a good rest to steady my shot. My heart was pounding, so I decided to take a front "boiler room" shot instead of my traditional neck shot. I touched off my shot and felt good about it. The elk wheeled away at impact and I knew we had him. Steve and I pursued after discussing a plan with Jim, who held back to see if we spooked anything else.

We hadn't walked ten steps in the direction of my elk when, *bang bang*! Two shots rang out. We got to a little rise minutes later and could see three guys standing over a bull elk that looked just like mine. Coincidence? I think not!

Then another shot split the air, but in the direction we left Jim. We got over to him and saw a wide smile of a friendly face. Jim had bagged a nice elk. After dressing out Jim's elk, we started the packing process. We bumped into the other guys packing out "my elk." They had hiked over the ridge from the salt water. They denied hearing my shot, or seeing an extra hole in "their elk." It is possible I missed, but I'm a pretty good shot and have killed enough game through the years to strongly reject their denials. Jim O was a hero on this hunt! He made sure we didn't go home empty-handed.

Steve's son, Sean, and my oldest son, Adam, are the same age and became great friends over the years. It was natural we would introduce them to hunting so they might "carry on the tradition." Neither of them are avid hunters today, but we had some good times when they did go. One such trip was up on the Denali Highway, caribou hunting. The boys were around 12 or so, and it wasn't a physical trip, as we had four-wheelers. We found a vantage point overlooking a valley and sat down. The weather was pretty crappy. As we glassed the panorama, the boys kind of got restless. I gave them the never-appreciated lecture of how patience is important, and you just never know when an animal might appear. Well, as if right on cue, Steve whispered, "Look, antlers!"

Sure enough, coming towards us, just at the curve of the hill below us, we could see a couple sets of antlers appearing as if growing from the ground. As the bodies of the caribou became visible, I tried to get Adam on one and Steve shot the other. The experience caused me to coin the phrase for the boys, "It only takes seconds to make a successful hunting trip out of an armed four-wheeler ride."

Chapter 10

"The Camp"

Kodiak Island is located roughly 420 miles south of Anchorage. Its largest city, also named Kodiak, has approximately 5400 residents and about the only commercial airport. Kodiak, the city, is one of the oldest communities in Alaska, having its roots in the Russian fur trade and being founded in 1792. We found ourselves having a long-term love affair with the place we called the camp on the south end of the island.

The rest of this chapter will contain snippets of stories from our 26-year history of hunting there. Each could probably be a chapter of its own, but the dates and all of the details have been blurred by time. One of our big mistakes through the years has been not journaling our adventures. So, let's get started!

My first trip to Kodiak with Steve was in 1989. Commercial air to the main town, and a chartered Grumman Goose Twin Engine Seaplane operated by Penn Air was the transportation method. We shipped most of our gear on northern air cargo and once we arrived we had the task of getting everything sorted in the hanger and loaded in the Goose. When we landed in the lagoon, the wind was blowing hard enough that, when the pilot turned to taxi to our beach, the wind caught one wing and tipped the plane up violently enough it poked the little porthole windows under the water on the downhill side. Fortunately, the pilot saw what was happening and applied throttle to get the plane facing back into the wind. Then he nursed the engines to hold us steady into the wind and let the wind push us to the beach backwards. On the same trip, on the way out, the weather was deteriorating and the clouds were dropping fast (Kodiak weather is always unpredictable). At one point, we were getting closer and closer to the ground and he hollered out above the engines, "If I can just make it over this next ridge, I think we'll be okay!"

Not what you want to hear your pilot say!

In 1921, reindeer were introduced to South Kodiak Island and the Alitak Native Reindeer Corporation was formed. The residents of the village of the Ahkiok managed the herd. The herd continued to grow through the '40s and reached about 3000 head by 1950. A wildfire in the early '50s destroyed much of the habitat in the area, and about 1200 of them escaped into the wild. Active management of the herd ended in 1961. By 1964, Fish and Game declared them feral and established hunting seasons with no bag limit. In 2010, Fish and Game restricted the season to six months and established a bag limit of one per hunter. They also officially reclassified them to caribou. The herd remains stable now at roughly 300 animals.

I told you all that to tell you that, on my first day at the camp, Steve stepped out of our cook shack and pointed up to the top of the first ridge, saying, "There they are, Stanley!"

He calls me Stanley a lot. I hate it, but what are friends for? I mean, when have you ever seen a guy named Stanley be a cool character in the movies?

Anyway, I looked up as far as I could with my cheap binoculars and saw what looked like black pepper spots on the new snow that fell at that elevation during the night. Steve said, "we can be there by noon and get your 'Boo."

It was my first trip there, so I agreed, maybe a bit too eagerly. The other hunters in camp decided to stay lower and hunt for deer, so off the two of us went. We made a direct assault on the face of the mountain since the herd of about 40 animals we saw had pushed over the top. We were out of sight, and the hike up was pretty much without note, except it was steep. My good buddy was off by 30 minutes or so. I squeezed the trigger around 11:30 AM. After dressing and bagging the respectable 'Boo, we ate lunch, enjoying the fantastic views that elevation gain rewards you with before spending the rest of the day packing back to camp. After dinner, we caped out the head for my shoulder mount.

Speaking about dinner, I think it's appropriate to talk about that here. When I first agreed to go on this hunt, I asked Steve whether I should bring freeze dried food I had left over from another hunt. He laughed at me and said sure. Then he told me I would be eating it alone because he "doesn't do freeze-dried." I was curious, then, what we would eat. Both Steve and I do most of the cooking in our respective households and have for years. I discovered that his belief is that there's no reason to deprive yourself just because you are hundreds of miles from home in a remote part of Alaska. Here is a standard menu from one of our trips to the camp in Steve's handwriting.

	MON	TUE	WED	THU	FRI	SAT	SUN/MON
BREAKFAST		Bacon, Eggs, Hash Brown	Oatmeal, English Muffin	Beer Batter Pancakes, Ham, Eggs	Oatmeal, English Muffin	Fr. Toast, Sausage, Eggs	Oatmeal, English Muffin
LUNCH / HOTDOGS		Pastrami Sandwich, Cookies, Candy Bar	Polish Sausage, Cheese, Ritz, Candy Bar	Roast Beef Sandwich, Cookies, M&M's	Polish Sausage, Cheese, Ritz, Apple & Cheeses	Ham & Cheese Sandwich, Cookies, Candy	Pastrami Sandwich, Candy, Apples
HOR D'OEUVRES	Chips & Salsa	Halibut Dip	Fr. Onion Dip, Potato Chips	Shrimp Cocktail Sauce	Chips & Dip	Shrimp	Scallop Stuffed Mushrooms
DINNER	Tacos, Spanish Rice, Refried Beans	Pork Chops, Mac & Cheese, Frozen Veg	Fresh Deer, Potatoes, Salad, Fr. Bread	Corn Beef & Cabbage, Potatoes, Carrots	Chicken & Dumplings, Salad, Potatoes, Corn	Fr. Rice, Egg Rolls, Sweet & Sour Pork	Steak, Potatoes, Brown Sauce, Mix Veg, Fr. Bread

We eat better in camp than our families do when we are gone! As the years progressed, the meals got more and more extravagant, trying to test the limits of what one can prepare with a propane cooktop and a wood stove. We have made escargot-stuffed Cajun-style mushrooms, chicken and dumplings, egg rolls, and other fare that you just don't get in every camp. Of course, there are also the special sauces that go with the meat. Every good cook knows it's all about the sauce. Jimmy O makes a delicious bordelaise sauce to go on fresh venison backstrap, as an example.

Now may be a good time to actually talk about the camp. We fly into a freshwater lagoon at the south end of Kodiak Island in a float plane. For the past 20 years, that has been with Seahawk Air pilot and owner Rolan Ruoss. We carry with us a chainsaw, propane tank, and stoves—both a wood stove and a cook stove. The first day is spent setting up camp. We build a specific style of structure out of driftwood found around the lagoon. It has to be tall enough for Steve and me. It also must be strong enough to withstand the notorious winds of the Shelikof Strait. Once the frame is up, we cover it with nylon reinforced plastic, the kind you see on construction sites stapled and secured with lath. The clear color allows for decent light inside. We build a kitchen counter on which we put the propane stove. We also have a small sheet metal wood-burning stove we install at one end, adding propane lanterns that hang from the rustic trusses, and you have it. A couple of our food boxes with a piece of plywood make up our kitchen table, surrounded by folding camp chairs. We probably violated some copyright and trade laws when we named this place the "Hilton."

We protect ourselves by putting up a battery operated electric bear fence to keep the big furry brown things out of our food. Outside the fence and a few good yards away are a row of tents we set up to act as our bedrooms. The location at the head of the lagoon by the creek allows us to have a reliable source of plenty of fresh water, when pumped through a filter. Several yards down the beach, we take advantage of a steep bank and extend a couple of driftwood logs out to make a tripod structure, and that supports our game pole. Covered with a tarp for rain, it provides lots of air flow so the meat cools out but yet is still protected from the ever-present Kodiak moisture. This we also string electric fencing around, so we don't lose any meat. The last chore of the day is to fire up the chainsaw and cut a week's worth of firewood. We would then stack this tightly into the "Hilton" so it can dry out. I have to say, the wood stove is the key part of this whole adventure. To be able to come back at the end of the day and get warm and dry, no matter the weather, is paramount to our success here.

Let's go back to hunting! The second day of my first visit, we were all headed up towards a place we called "the Bowl." It is one of the closest serious hunts we do and is about an hour away. I was trudging along near the back of the pack when Steve said, "There's a pretty nice buck, Stan, do you want him?"

Boom!

I didn't even have the chance to fully process what I'd heard before this nice three by three buck was on the ground. I looked at my buddy incredulously and he just smiled and said, "Don't worry, there will be more."

I guess I was thinking about moose hunting, or perhaps deer, in other states, where you can be considered lucky to even see a single deer. Here, on my first hunt, the limit was five each! Depending on the winter kill, it gets adjusted up or down, but after the last five years or so, the limit has averaged to steady three per year per hunter.

I suppose it would be a good time to discuss geography. At least, our names for the terrain around the camp. Most every hunter has that special place they slap some moniker on so that only people known to the hunt will know what he's talking about. We are no exception. All the references about direction here will be as if you were standing on the beach of the lagoon, looking at the Hilton. On the right side, you have The Bowl, The Cut, Around the Rim, The Face, The Chute, The Beaver Pond, and Around the Horn. On the left side, we recognize the Big Valley, The Hog Back, Elephant Buck Valley, and Valley of the Moon.

As mentioned before, "The Bowl" is located about an hour's walk and two creek crossings away on the right. Mostly forested by slide alders on the left and dotted with patches of wild raspberries in the middle, it was wide open and grassy on the right. On the right, also at the ridgeline, is a ravine that runs almost a third of the way down into the ridge, making access to the top of a ridge a little easier. That ravine is "The Cut," and once you attain elevation, you could walk much more easily "Around the Rim," which is the ridge line that surrounds The Bowl. After you make it all the way around, you need to drop back down to the valley floor, using "The Chute" to get through the thick stuff and the steep descent. Before you drop down The Chute, 50 or so yards to your right is a small bowl on the next mountain over, which is "The Face." That mountain, at its base, after passing the Beaver Pond and turning the corner to where you have a clear view of Halibut Bay, is called "Around the Horn."

On the other side of the lagoon, closest to the saltwater, is the "Big Valley," and about halfway up on the left is the "Hog Back," which is a ridge that sticks out of the side of the valley and makes access to the top a little less steep. The next valley is "Elephant Buck Valley," so named by our friend, Jimmy O, because of the big buck he saw way in the back of it, but couldn't get close enough for a shot. Quite a ways further inland is the "Valley of The Moon," which is no valley at all. Actually, it is a ridge that we walk up the backside of because it is void of vegetation and mostly solid dirt and gravel. Not having to fight the alders and brush is a huge advantage. The primary disadvantage is that you stick out like a sore thumb while you hike up. I think there is mineral there the deer like, since we almost always see them there. "The Flats" are the big wide open area between these mountains. Flying in, they look flat, but, in reality, they are anything but. Filled with sharp cuts and small ridges, they provide deer and caribou with lots of ways to make the passage from one side of our area to the other without detection.

I told you all that to tell a few stories about the places that made them memorable. I'll start with one about a good friend who probably wouldn't want me to mention him by name here (OZ). We were paired up one day and decided to walk up the cut and around the rim. We saw a few small bucks and a lot of does on the way, but nothing we wanted to settle for that early in the hunt, so we trudged and glassed along our way around The Rim. After eating lunch from our lofty perch with a great view of the valley below and the Shelikof Strait in the distance, my buddy lights up a cigarette. I'm not one to judge, since I smoke my cigars, but when he lit the second one, I said, "Hey, you better knock that off. The elevation up here may get to you."

He said something like, "I don't inhale, so it's no big deal."

So, off we go after he finishes that one and I finish my caramel apple (Years before, my pal Steve taught me to bite half of a Kraft caramel with a bite of apple. As you chew them together, it tastes just like a caramel apple you get at the fair, but a lot less messy).

Anyway, we walked about another 15 minutes and were rewarded with a good look at three bucks a little too far away to shoot. I laid a plan to go after them and my buddy said he was ready. After another five minutes on the trail, I felt a sharp tug on my backpack, stopping me in my tracks. My friend who doesn't inhale said, "I've got to get off of here!"

Curious, as I looked into his pale face, I asked him if he couldn't hold off for just a bit more since we were almost in shooting position. The look on his face was my answer. Well, crap! I offered to rope to him, but he didn't think it was necessary if he could just follow close and hang on to my pack as we walked. With empty packs, we headed down. I was not happy. I had to pass on a nice buck, and I had a dizzy guy pulling and pushing on my pack all the way down the steep descent of The Chute.

As soon as we hit the relatively flat ground, he spins me around with the death grip he has on my pack and says, "Whatever you do, don't tell Steve!"

I promised I wouldn't, but these things always get out among friends. It was my turn in the kitchen for appetizers that day, so I'm in there, working away, preparing our scallop stuffed Cajun mushrooms, singing the old song from the late 60s, "Dizzy (pa pa pah), I'm so dizzy, my head is spinning, like a whirlpool, it never ends . . ." You may know the song.

Over my voice, I heard my buddy, who swore me to secrecy, yell, "Tebow, you told him, didn't you?"

Steve just looked at him and said, "Told me what?"

I laughed as our good buddy spilled the whole story! You just can't make this stuff up.

I knew he'd spill his guts, because a similar thing happened on his first trip with us. His wife made him bring a can of pepper spray for protection. In a camp with experienced hunters and magnum rifles, he brings an aerosol can of pepper spray. On one of the first days, he was paired with our friend Bob Thompson and lost said can of pepper spray. After employing Bob to look for it for half an hour or so, the same promise was solicited. "Don't tell Flascher!"

As you can guess by now, it wasn't long that night at dinner before out comes, "Thompson, you told him, didn't you?"

Steve looked up from his steak and asked, "Told me what?"

After the story came out, the teasing started, with Bob expertly setting the stage. He asked, "What were you going to do with a can of pepper spray, anyway?"

He spun his hat around backwards and pointed his nonexistent can at the make-believe bear, and said, "Come on mother f—r! Come on!! Pssst! Psst!"

We laughed until we cried.

I should tell you just one more story about this guy, primarily because he had a very good way of providing such good material. I lived in Anchorage at the time, and my neighbor was a friend I met through my wife. Our wives worked together. His name was Dana, and he was an accountant for the Sheraton hotel. Dana talked about hunting when he was a kid in Michigan, so I invited him to go to Kodiak with us. That particular trip, we had a full camp, so we set off as a trio. We weren't too far from camp when a pretty nice buck jumped up. When they are close to camp, they don't have to be big to be targeted, just respectable, and this one was nice enough.

Dana whispered to me, "Can I shoot it?"

I said, "No, it's not your turn."

Our other friend, yeah, the pepper spray guy, let off a shot. Nothing. *Bang! Bang!* Reload, *bang* again. Finally, he hit the deer in the right front foot. The deer started to jump up and dance.

Dana, who wears glasses as thick as coke bottles, kindly put the deer out of his misery with a clean shot through the heart. After we got back to camp, we paced off 100 yards and set up a paper plate with a bullseye. Our buddy, who complained all day about how the flight must have knocked his scope off, now was laying on the ground for stability. He touches off his 7mm magnum and drills the bullseye dead center. I told him with a knowing grin, "I'd have pulled that one on purpose if I had been you." Now we knew it wasn't the gun.

My buddy Steve has a reputation for having good luck. Now, I admit, he's a hell of a hunter, but, well, as his dad used to tell him, "better lucky than good." We were headed up The Bowl one day. It was one of my first trips, because we hadn't discovered Swarovski optics yet. We jumped a buck that took off running up the wide open hillside next to the cut. I pulled up as it was my turn to shoot that morning. Nothing but fog in my scope! I grabbed my ever-present bandana to clear the fog, but the buck was getting away. I hollered out to Steve, "Don't wait for me."

He laid down, folded down his bipod, boom! The buck rolled down to within 50 yards of us. Steve had hit him in the head at 400 yards running. Skill? Yeah, maybe, but I believe in good old luck sometimes. The nickname Rambuck was born!

One year, we took off as a group of four, which is not unusual. We'd spot deer in different directions, then split into pairs. This particular day, we were still together when we were almost to the top of The Hog Back into Big Valley. Steve and I were in the lead, being the senior members. We crouched further and further down as we crested the ridge to avoid skylighting ourselves, and we're pleasantly surprised to see two nice bucks feeding right towards us. We crept back down our side of the ridge a few yards and motioned to our buddies to be quiet. The bucks crested the ridge and, through our regular unspoken understanding of each other, I took the one on the right, Steve took the one on the left. Both shots rang out as one. Both deer dropped in their tracks. I like neck shots close to the base of a skull. Steve likes headshots. Neither ruin much, if any, meat. My shot allows for just a little more room for error, I believe. Which might be important if you aren't that good. Well, after we shot, we heard the funniest noise. It was the antler from Steve's deer *whoop whoop whooping* as it spun through the air.

Another time found my friend Dana and I way back in the Big Valley, looking at a nice buck too late in the day. I squeezed the trigger at 4:30 PM. Dana already had a nice buck in his pack. As we dressed my deer out, a red fox kept getting closer and braver, snapping his teeth and whining at us. He got a little too close for comfort, so I shot him, too, and we skinned him out. Now loaded, we started back, questioning my judgment. It was 8:30 PM and pitch dark when we finally got back to the Hilton. The last several hundred yards were illuminated by the strong flashlights of our buddies in camp. Corned beef and cabbage with potatoes and carrots never tasted so good, which was followed by the good-natured ribbing that worried friends come up with. Mostly just, "What the heck were you doing/thinking?" As I write this, I am able to look over my shoulder and see the mount of this buck, one of the three I have done from all of the deer we have been blessed with from this great place.

As you know by now, we were landing on a freshwater lagoon separated from the Shelikof Strait by a narrow gravel spit. Every now and then, the water in the lagoon gets deep enough, and conditions right enough, that the gravel washes out to the ocean and the lagoon becomes tidal again. Well, this action has led to a varying mix of fish being present. We never fished it, but Steve's sons-in-law are fanatical fishermen, especially Jeremy. He would put in a full day in the field hunting, sometimes walking several miles back with a pack loaded with deer meat, then grab a fishing pole and fish until it got dark. The fish looked like smaller, land-locked salmon but a tad green in color. In all our years, we never tried to eat one.

Steve, Jeremy, Rob, and I were headed Around the Horn one day when we saw a deer run through a clearing just in front of us.

Right behind him was a huge brown bear loping at full speed. It was very surprising, and the bear, as he ran, turned his head our way, gave us an evil eye, then continued his pursuit without breaking stride. It was a vision that took just a split, but was burned into our memories forever.

In September of 2012, Steve's friend Greg Svendsen came to The Camp. Greg is an avid hunter, but early in his time in camp, he pulled a groin muscle badly carrying a loaded pack. We called the plane back to pick him up. He was lucky, in a way. The very next day, we woke up to 8 inches of heavy, wet snow and proceeded to have some of the worst weather we've ever encountered there. That year, James also brought his son, Jake, to Kodiak. Jake has some food allergy issues, and I remember Steve saying James would just have to bring the stuff for Jake. In typical Steve style, though, we unpacked the groceries he bought and there was gluten free pasta, bread, and the like, as well as special hot dogs Jake could eat. He cooked separate meals for him. We had a great week and, as I remember it, everyone limited out with three deer each. Jake was 15 years old.

One year, it finally happened!

"**What**?" Steve asked.

I said, "I have some friends I'd like to bring to Kodiak for our annual hunt. Brian and Leslie . . ."

"Whoa, a woman in camp, no way! We can't be held back. It's a tough hunt—" yadda, yadda, yadda . . .

"But Steve, she's a sheep hunter and has a real nice mountain goat as well." I'm planning on bringing them.

"Well, okay," he said, not terribly happy with me.

I met Brian and Leslie through my wife, Judy, when they were all nurses at the local hospital in town. We became friends and shared many hunting stories, but this was our first and only hunt together.

It turned out to be great fun, but first, let's talk about facilities. There aren't any! We take a piece of plywood with a hole in it and build a crude toilet seat. This gets nailed to a couple of logs over a hole we dig. All of it a few yards from camp, in a direct wind off the Shelikof Strait. No cover, no shelter, no privacy.

Leslie handled it like the seasoned pro she is. She never complained about the wet, windy conditions and we always respected her privacy. No photos of bare butts, like some of our other guests through the years. She and Brian were great in camp, worked hard, and quickly became valued members of our hunt. In fact, on the first day, we went quite a ways and Leslie made a terrific shot on a nice buck at 158 yards. I remember the distance, because Brian, in his good-natured way, asked me how far I thought it was as he dug out his range finder. I looked and took a half-hearted guess at 155 yards. He was amazed and I think I earned some respect I didn't deserve. I was just guessing.

On one of the days, we went Around the Horn, and as I've mentioned, it's one of the longer walks we do. Leslie and I both shot nice bucks, but mine didn't tumble to the bottom, so Brian and I went up after it. Once we got up to where it was, Brian realized we were pretty close to the top, so he decided to "take a look." I dragged my deer down to where Steve and Leslie were working on her deer. We got both deer bagged and we were a little bit worried about Brian when he appeared on the skyline. You could have seen his smile from a mile away. He got down to us and announced it was the best day of deer hunting he's had in his life.

Brian and Leslie are always welcome at our campfire. Not everyone is. We've had a couple of real jerks through the years, but their stories won't be told here.

Back in the early days, maybe the fourth or fifth year, we invited Brian Cain to Kodiak with us—the same Brian who was on our second Farewell bison hunt. We also accidentally had some leftover fireworks mixed up with our hunting gear. I'm pretty sure there was some discussion about noise to scare bears and some such thing, but no bears had come close to camp. The last night of a hunt requires that we celebrate our successful outing. The problem was that the wind was blowing like 50 miles an hour, gusting to 75 miles an hour! I'm just guessing, of course, but darn, if it wasn't whistling. In fact, it was blowing so hard the box of ten mortar rounds turned over to face us as the first one ignited. As we dove for cover behind a huge driftwood log, you could hear Brian yell over the noise of the wind, "You just gotta love it!" as the fireworks flew by!

One year, after the limit on deer was reduced to three deer, four of us headed to the Valley of the Moon on the first day of the hunt. As mentioned before, The Flats aren't really flat, and between camp and the Valley of the Moon, there's a pretty large ravine that you can go around or cut through. We always stopped there to glass for deer, as it's a major escape route for them moving from one canyon to another. This particular day, we approached the edge carefully and saw a nice three by three buck—a six-pointer, for our East Coast friends—feeding by the small stream at the bottom. Not a huge buck, but respectable. We glanced around at each other and nobody else seemed to be interested, so I shot him. Down he goes!

I racked another round and darned if the thing didn't get back up, so I shot again. Down in the willows he fell, again. My buddies are starting to put packs back on and move on when one of them yelled at me and pointed. That darn buck is standing, looking right at me!

One more time, confidence shaken, I took careful aim from a solid rest across my pack with my bipod extended. Bam! The buck dropped instantly. I took a little ribbing from my friends as they took off walking. It was decided I could dress this deer out and get it back to camp myself, since it was early in the day. I gathered up my spent brass and headed to collect my deer.

I was a bit surprised when I arrived and found that not only one buck lay on the ground, but three. They all looked exactly the same! I whistled at the guys and they came to help out. So, if you're keeping track, I tagged out in the first three hours of our week-long hunt. I spent the rest of the hunt packing for my friends. That's how it goes sometimes.

Every now and then, a life-changing event jumps up and grabs you. In September of 2006, that happened to me. Steve and I had just taken all of our gear to Northern Air Cargo and shipped it to Kodiak for our annual hunt. I was on my way home to Wasilla and decided to stop by my office building. I had recently paid a painter to paint and he had announced the day before, Saturday, that he was done. I thought I'd swing by and check his work. I discovered he had completed the painting, but he hadn't put the storm windows back in, so I ran home and grabbed my extension ladder and went back in the rain that had started to fall. On the last window of the second story dormer, the ladder decides to take a slide across the wet grass. I fell roughly 14 feet, landing on my left side. Final tally of broken bones looked like this: both collarbones, both shoulder blades, five ribs, a split sternum, and one punctured lung thrown in for fun. I missed the hunting trip that year. Steve and Jimmy O took a boat hunt out of Kodiak instead.

In 2011, we had Steve's two sons-in-law in camp. It was Rob's first trip with us. Jeremy had been there before. There are a few pockets of mountain goats on Kodiak island. For residents, a simple registration tag and some serious guts are all that is necessary to hunt these Snow White goats. After my fall, I had a few years during which I couldn't do much physically, but by 2011, I was fired up and ready to take this on. Nobody, in all our years, had gone after a goat. I came prepared to "spike out" and have a tough night if it was necessary to get close to one. James Buchanon, who I've known since he was ten years old, said he'd go with me, but he thought we should go light and fast rather than carry an extra camp. I decided to do it his way and, the next morning, we were on our way before daybreak. Steve almost came but James had piped up first.

James and I made good time as we went to The Bowl and topped out on The Cut shortly after sunup. From there, it was ridgetop hiking. I've always been amazed at how easy it is to walk up there after working so hard to get there. We took The Rim until we met a crossing ridge that would take us closer to where the goats hang out. We figured we'd be able to spot them from above and then come up with a plan.

That's almost exactly what happened. We were on top of the third ridge back when James asked me what that was way down in the bottom, near the salt water. My first thought was a very blonde brown bear. We swiftly dug out our binoculars and sat down for a better look. It was white; it was a goat! It was also headed up the valley from our right to our left, probably a mile away.

At that time, we decided to wait and see for a bit what his intentions were. Since we were at the top of the ridge and goats like lofty places, it seemed like a good idea. He kept coming and we kept watching. When he crossed beneath our position as it related to the valley floor, he turned uphill, but not on the ridge we were on. It was on the one we had passed to get to the one we were on. As the goat rounded a small hill on the ridge he was climbing and we were out of sight, we jumped up. James and I came to some sort of silent agreement, because we threw our packs on as quickly as possible and took off running. The advantage of being at the top of the mountain is that it isn't as far around it as it is at the base. We were able to use this advantage and get above the spot where we thought Mr. Shaggy was going to show up.

After a few minutes, we started second guessing ourselves and slowly split up to peek over the edge. When we were about 30 yards apart, the goat appeared right in front of us. As we made eye contact, he wheeled to run, but it was too late. After photos, we ate lunch and dressed the goat out for a life-sized mount. The hair on these creatures is the real trophy. Loaded with all the meat, entire head, and hide, we made our way back to camp. As we stopped at the meat pole, the others were there also hanging up the deer and caribou that Steve and Jeremy shot up in the Big Valley. Steve could see we were loaded, so he hollered out, "What did you get?"

He was surprised when the snow white goat hide came out of my pack. We all told stories about our day and Rob walked over to me first, then James and Steve, shaking our hands vigorously. Then he stepped back and said, "I can't believe you old f—rs have been doing this for over 20 years."

It is not for the faint of heart.

Another short story worth mentioning. My father, Jim, came to our camp two weeks before his 70th birthday. He had trouble getting around on the tundra and didn't get a deer, but it was great to have him in camp. Stories of his hunting trips from the old days entertained our evenings. His teaching got me out there, and I'm glad we could have a chance to share a special camp with him. For the record, as I write this in 2024, we are planning a moose hunt with Dad again, and he is almost 90. More on moose in a different chapter titled Moose Camp.

When my son was a sophomore in high school, he came to camp, too. He got a nice buck and Steve, who was paired up with him that day, packed it back for him. One year, shortly after I started going to the camp, I remembered Steve, Dana, James, and I had been out together when Steve shot a buck that rolled down the backside of a ridge. Away from camp! He told us to stay on top to see if we could see more to get, then it started to snow. As I was glassing the hills and valleys around, I saw movement through the snow. It didn't take a genius to see it was a huge brown bear. It wouldn't have bothered me too much, except it was about 300 yards from where Steve was elbow deep in the blood of a fresh kill. The bear stood up, sniffed the air and headed straight for Steve, who couldn't see him due to the terrain. In fact, he was concentrating on his job at hand.

I started down to help watch over my buddy, hollering and waving my arms. The bear turned around and wandered off when I was still 50 yards away. At that point, I continued to the kill site and helped Steve finish what little work he had left. He never saw the bear and wondered why I came down to help.

There are more stories, of course, but time and details are mixed. I do not know the exact number, but, between Steve and I alone, we figure we have taken at least 100 bucks out of this area in the years we've hunted there. My last trip to The Camp was in 2018, and Steve's son-in-law, Rob, was back in camp. We also had a treat in that, having the gender restriction broken by Leslie, Steve's daughter, Kelly, also was there. We had a great week, with Rob and Kelly putting in the work and getting the big bucks we used to get. The torch has passed.

This from Steve:

One of the great days of this hunt was the last day. Rob and Kelly were headed toward the Valley of the Moon and Stan and I were hunting the face of Elephant Buck Valley. Stan and I didn't see any bucks where we were hunting, so we started hiking over to where we last saw Rob and Kelly. As we approached the valley, we could see them glassing up the left ridge. We knew they were looking at a deer, and Kelly finally grabbed her rifle. After getting a good rest, she started looking through her scope and it was a long, long time before she pulled the trigger on her rifle. She had shot her first buck (3 by 3) with one shot right through the heart. She was really excited and was giving Rob hugs when another buck stood up about 150 yards away. She said, "What should we do?" and Rob said, "Shoot it."

She grabbed her rifle and again drilled her second buck with another one shot kill. Needless to say, we all had full packs to carry back to camp. What a day. It really meant a lot for me to be there along with Kelly, Rob, and Stan in a place that has been so special to me for 20 plus years. The torch has been passed!

Grant Lagoon from "The Rim"

Grant Lagoon looking towards the "Big Valley"

James B taking a break

The Camp!

Rambuck is born!

The Hilton!

We decided to pack three

Jimmy O hiking up the Valley of the Moon

My first 'Boo

Kelly's deer

Brian Stan and Steve

Brian with the sattelite dish anters Farewell 2nd trip

Chris Marok with Halibut

OZ took an 80 mile cab ride for these

Stan an Jim Tebow at The Camp

Stan and Adam on top

Steve with my 63 inch antlers Farewell first trip

The Lil' Sprout

The Camp
by Stan Tebow

The planning starts early, it's on the phone.
The menu is extraordinary but not done.
There's corned beef and cabbage, and chicken with dumplin's
There's shrimp and egg rolls and brown sauce for fixin's.
There's one night of Mexican and one of Oriental,
But the taste buds are watering for the venison special.
To the camp!
Each man has his list so as not to forget
The very item when not there, would make him fret.
The socks are even counted and matched in pairs
The spare clothes, first aid, and rifles are packed with care.
The sleeping bags and tents, the packs with supplies
Are gathered and readied for the long exciting flight.
To the camp!
As the countdown continues we drive friends and family mad,
With stories upon stories of past trips that we've had.
We call with regularity ones who have been before
And ask if they would like to go just once more.
Unless you've been, it might be hard to understand,
The grip that it holds on you, this land.
To the camp!
It's almost time to go, what's a "git-up" anyway?
We are all ready and waiting for our seven day stay.
Then it's commercial air to Kodiak, and small plane from then on.
We rock with the turbulence and hope for the sun.
As the plane gets nearer and we look with anticipation
For the camp!

The gear is unloaded and packed to the shore.
We are happy at this time we didn't take more.
The real fun begins now with pick up and clean up:
Then there's wood to cut, tents to set, all before sup.
You see, the morning will start with a steep, steep climb.
The realization has hit us all, we've arrived
At the camp!
The days pass quickly, each one with a story,
Look now! Up on that ridge, a huge buck in full glory!
We climb and we sweat in an effort to get near.
The mountain gets stepper, the buck looks down with a sneer.
As we approach the top with our butts dragging,
He's gone and there's no need in lagging,
Back to camp.
We've had many a good trip; in and out once more on time.
We know the day will come when we can only pine.
When the hills are too steep and the deer are too scarce.
When our legs will fail us and the chase is a farce.
But until that day be sure we'll keep coming
To the special place that keeps our hearts drumming.
The camp!

Conclusion

I hope you have enjoyed our stories.

One of my biggest mistakes and regrets is that we didn't keep accurate notes on any of our trips. There are so many more stories that would be fun reading, but we couldn't come up with the details because we didn't write them down.

Now that we are older gentlemen, there is not likely going to be a second installment of this book, but we will keep trying to make more exciting memories. Perhaps guided trips from here on out, where young, athletic folks can do what we took for granted so long ago! . . . Hmmm, there may be stories coming up that are worth telling!

Review Inquiry

Hey, it's Stan Tebow here.

I hope you've enjoyed the book, finding it both useful and fun. I have a favor to ask you.

Would you consider giving it a rating wherever you bought the book? Online book stores are more likely to promote a book when they feel good about its content, and reader reviews are a great barometer for a book's quality.

So please go to the website of wherever you bought the book, search for my name and the book title, and leave a review. If able, perhaps consider adding a picture of you holding the book. That increases the likelihood your review will be accepted!

Many thanks in advance,
Stan Tebow

About the Author

Stan Tebow is a seasoned insurance professional with over four decades of experience serving clients in Anchorage, Alaska, and the surrounding region. A masterful storyteller, he has seamlessly woven his passion for hunting narratives into his professional interactions. Currently residing in Northern Idaho with his wife, Judy, and their two English Bulldogs, Stan remains actively engaged in sales training and continues to maintain his insurance practice. An avid traveler and dedicated grandparent, he balances professional commitments with rich personal experiences that inform his approach to business and life.

Stan can be reached at: stan.tebow@gmail.com

www.ingramcontent.com/pod-product-compliance
Lightning Source LLC
Chambersburg PA
CBHW061658120626
46550CB00003B/1001